Relish
NORTH EAST & YORKSHIRE

Original recipes from the regions' best-loved chefs and restaurants. Introduction by chef patron Michael Wignall.

First Published 2019
By Relish Publications
Shield Green Farm, Tritlington,
Northumberland, NE61 3DX.

Twitter: @Relish_Cookbook
Facebook: RelishRestaurantGuide
Instagram: Relish_Cookbook
For cookbooks and recipes visit:
www.relishpublications.co.uk
For publishing enquiries visit:
www.relish-publishing.co.uk

ISBN: 978-0-9934678-8-2

Publisher: Duncan L Peters
General Manager: Teresa Peters
Design: Vicki Brown
Proofing Coordinator: Valerie McLeod
Relish Photography: Nicky Rogerson
Editorial Consultant: Paul Robertson
Twitter: @paulrobbo1966

Front cover photograph by: Nicholas Bennett
www.nicholasbennettdop.com

Printed in Poland on behalf of Latitude Press.

Relish
PUBLICATIONS

Welcome to this third edition of Relish North East and Yorkshire, with a mouthwatering selection of recipes from the regions' best-loved chefs and restaurants. We know you will enjoy visiting or cooking your way through the pages of this carefully curated collection.

Relish Publications began life in 2009 when two food lovers and experienced publishers (Duncan and Teresa) unfolded a new concept in recipe books, which reflect the same attention to detail and care that our featured chefs deliver, each and every day.

We have circumnavigated the UK in our hunt for the most highly acclaimed eateries, hidden gems and those highly recommended by other best-loved chefs in the UK.

We invite you to join our Relish community on Instagram, Facebook and Twitter. We love to hear from our readers and so do the Relish chefs.

Best wishes

Duncan and Teresa Peters

004
CONTENTS

015 FOREWORD BY CHEF MICHAEL WIGNALL

016 1910 STEAK & SEAFOOD
Spanish City, Spanish City Plaza, Whitley Bay, Tyne & Wear, NE26 1BG. T: 0191 691 7090
www.spanishcity.co.uk/1910-steak-seafood

026 ACKLAM HALL
Hall Drive, Acklam, Middlesbrough, TS5 7DY. T: 01642 822 000 www.acklamhall.co.uk

036 THE ANGEL AT HETTON
The Angel Inn, Hetton, Skipton, BD23 6LT. T: 01756 730 263 www.angelhetton.co.uk

046 BROCKLEY HALL BOUTIQUE HOTEL & RESTAURANT
Glenside, Saltburn-by-the-Sea, TS12 1JS. T: 01287 622 179 www.brockleyhallhotel.com

056 THE BRUCE ARMS
Main Street, West Tanfield, Ripon, North Yorkshire, HG4 5JJ. T: 01677 470 325 www.thebrucearms.com

066 CAFE LILLI
83 Norton High Street, Norton, TS20 1AE. T: 01642 554 422 www.lillicafe.co.uk

076 COLMANS SEAFOOD TEMPLE
Sea Road, South Shields, NE33 2LD. T: 0191 511 1349 www.colmansseafoodtemple.co.uk

086 DOXFORD HALL HOTEL & SPA
Chathill, Alnwick, Northumberland, NE67 5DN. T: 01665 589 700 www.doxfordhall.com

096 ESHOTT HALL
Eshott Hall, Morpeth, Northumberland, NE65 9EN. T: 01670 787 454 www.eshotthall.co.uk

106 HEADLAM HALL
Headlam, Near Gainford, Darlington, DL2 3HA. T: 01325 730 238 www.headlamhall.co.uk

116 THE JOLLY FISHERMAN
Haven Hill, Craster, Northumberland, NE66 3TR. T: 01665 576 461 www.thejollyfishermancraster.co.uk

132 LOLLO ROSSO
40 Bridge Street, Morpeth, NE61 1NL. T: 01670 514 111 www.lollorossoitalia.com

006
CONTENTS

142 THE ORANGERY AT ROCKLIFFE HALL
Rockliffe Hall, Hurworth on Tees, Darlington, County Durham, DL2 2DU. T: 01325 729 999
www.rockliffehall.com

152 PEACE & LOAF
217 Jesmond Road, Newcastle upon Tyne, NE2 1LA. T: 0191 281 5222 www.peaceandloaf.co.uk

162 THE PIPE & GLASS
West End, South Dalton, East Yorkshire, HU17 7PN. T: 01430 810 246 www.pipeandglass.co.uk

172 THE ROSE & CROWN AT ROMALDKIRK
Barnard Castle, County Durham, DL12 9EB. T: 01833 650 213 www.rose-and-crown.co.uk

182 SHIBDEN MILL INN
Shibden Mill Fold, Shibden, Halifax, HX3 7UL. T: 01422 365 840 www.shibdenmillinn.com

192 THE VIOLET GREEN
68a The Green, Norton, TS20 1BN. T: 01642 533 006 www.thevioletgreen.co.uk

202 WALWICK HALL HOTEL & COUNTRY ESTATE
Walwick Hall, Humshaugh, Hexham, Northumberland, NE46 4BJ. T: 01434 620 156 www.walwickhall.com

212 THE WENSLEYDALE HEIFER HOTEL & RESTAURANT
West Witton, Leyburn, DL8 4LS. T: 01969 622 322 www.wensleydaleheifer.co.uk

222 THE WESTWOOD RESTAURANT
New Walk, Beverley, East Yorkshire, HU17 7AE. T: 01482 881 999 www.thewestwood.co.uk

232 LARDER

240 GLOSSARY

242 RELISH ALL THE INGREDIENTS

244 RELISH AVAILABLE TO BUY

246 HINTS & TIPS

247 CONVERSION CHART

King Scallops, Chicken Skin Custard, Strawberries, Ver Jus, Dukkah Spice - **Page 186**

009
STARTERS

020   Cured Salmon, Smoked Salmon Mousse, Burnt Apple, Lemon, Dill Oil

030   Charred Mackerel, Horseradish, Beetroot

040   Yorkshire Dales Poultry Pressing, Pheasant Liver Parfait, Celery Gel

050   Rabbit Ballotine, Heritage Carrots, Capers, Raisins, Sherry Vinegar

060   Sautéed Tiger Prawns & Squid with Lemon, Herbs, Tomato & Garlic Butter Sauce, Parmesan Tuile

070   Beetroot, Pickled Shallots, Horseradish Jelly, Pink Gnocchi, Goat's Cheese Snow

080   Smoked Mackerel Pâté

090   Local Goat's Curd, Textures of Beetroot, Savoury Granola

100   Pigeon, Scotch Egg, Beetroot

110   Salted Cod, Butternut Velouté, Pickled Butternut

120   Kipper Scotch Egg, Truffle Mayonnaise

122   'Posh Pea & Ham Soup', Ham Hock, Pistachio & Mustard Terrine, Pea Velouté, Pease Pudding

136   Insalata Calda Di Mare

146   Asparagus with Harissa

156   Torched Mackerel, Blood Orange, Carrot, Coastal Herbs

166   Crab, Carrot & Coriander Salad, Toasted Hazelnuts, Sea Salt Flatbread

176   Tempura Monkfish with Vadouvan Spice, Mushy Peas, Tartare Sauce Hollandaise

186   King Scallops, Chicken Skin Custard, Strawberries, Ver Jus, Dukkah Spice

196   Octopus, Hoisin Pork Belly, Pickled Rhubarb

206   Poached Organic Salmon & Herb Ballotine, Saffron Mayonnaise, Granola, Caperberry

216   Chilli Salt Squid

226   Cep Mushroom & Jerusalem Artichoke Macaroni, Arlington White Hen's Egg, Autumn Black Truffle

011
MAINS

022   Pavé of Halibut, Compressed Cucumber, Shellfish Broth, Sea Herbs

032   Duo of Neesham Beef

042   Yorkshire Partridge, Boudin Noir Purée, Game Jus

052   North Atlantic Cod, Langoustine, Crosnes, Rainbow Kale, Smoked Cod Roe Emulsion

062   Crispy Breast of West Tanfield Lamb, Creamy Chive Mash, Wilted Brassicas, Baby Carrots, Red Wine & Port Jus

072   Pan Fried Cod, Polenta Mousse, Malaysian Chilli Sauce

082   Pan Roast Hake, Garlic Prawns, Braised Chorizo in Red Wine

084   Salmon Teriyaki, Stir Fried Asian Vegetables

092   Pan Roasted John Dory, Oxtail Croquette, Pumpkin, Split Pumpkin Seed Jus

102   Turbot

112   Pan Fried Breast of Duck, Fig Purée, Red Cabbage, Roast Baby Carrots, Potato Laces, Citrus & Tarragon Jus

124   Asian Spiced Hake, Curry Mayonnaise, Spinach, Cauliflower Fritter, Bhaji, Bombay Potato

126   Beef Fillet, Wild Mushroom Risotto & Gratin, Confit Garlic, Onion Purée

138   Lobster Thermidor

148   Squab Pigeon, Chervil Root Dashi, Mushroom Ketchup

158   Rack of Lamb, White Asparagus, Razor Clam, Wild Garlic

168   Salt Beef Hash Cake, Fried Quail Egg, Rhubarb Ketchup, Pickled Onion Rings

178   Butter Poached Fillet of Joe Simpson's Beef, Roast Bone Marrow, Crispy Tongue, Braised Ox Cheek

188   Stone Bass, Caramelised Cauliflower Purée, Roasted Cauliflower, Parisienne Potatoes, Smoked Almonds, Parmesan Foam

198   Fillet of Blackwell's Beef with Hornleys Sauce

208   Roast Haunch of Venison, Textures of Beetroot, Kale, Bitter Chocolate Sauce

218   Sea Bass, Warm Salad of Chorizo & New Potatoes

228   Loin of Fallow Deer, Red Cabbage, Roasted Cereal & Grains, Brassicas, Game Jus, Blackberries

Forest Floor, Cherry, Pistachio, Itakuja – **Page 160**

013
DESSERTS

024 Baked Custard, Salted Crumble, Blackberry Sorbet

034 Baked Cinnamon Crème Brûlée, Rum & Raisin

044 'Snickers'- Peanut Parfait, Salted Caramel, Chocolate, Milk

054 Brockley Hall's own Lemon Top, Lemonade Parfait, Buckwheat Tuile

064 Passion Fruit Cheesecake with Granola Base & Passion Fruit Jelly Top

074 Salted Caramel Fondant

094 Lemon Crème Brûlée, Toasted Pine Nut Pastry, Earl Grey Tea Meringue

104 Fig Strudel

114 Chocolate & Marmalade Fondant

128 Sticky Toffee Pudding, Butterscotch Sauce, Vanilla Pod Ice Cream, Little Toffee Apples

130 Glazed Lemon Tart, Chocolate Ganache, Clotted Cream & Amaretto Milkshake

140 Tiramisu

150 Gariguette Strawberry, Estate Fennel

160 Forest Floor, Cherry, Pistachio, Itakuja

170 Dark Chocolate Honeycomb Bites

180 Chocolate Falcon, Pistachio, Blackberry

190 Shibden's Snickers

200 Peanut Butter Mousse, Banana, Raspberry

210 Milk Chocolate & Figs Dacquoise

220 Rhubarb & Custard Panna Cotta, Rhubarb Ripple Ice Cream

230 Chocolate Tart, Raspberries, Pistachio Brittle

015
FOREWORD BY MICHAEL WIGNALL

The north and I have history. It's where my roots are and where my career began - working with Paul Heathcote, first at Broughton, and then his famous restaurant in Longridge. Yorkshire is where I earned my first Michelin star at the Burlington Restaurant at the Devonshire Arms.

Since then, I've meandered down south, to The Latymer at Pennyhill Park and Gidleigh Park, before recently returning to Yorkshire in partnership with James Wellock, of fresh produce wholesaler Wellocks. We've taken over the famous Angel Inn at Hetton - the UK's first and original gastro-pub. Next year we'll be launching a fine dining restaurant across the road from The Angel. Cove will be my first restaurant and I'm excited and proud to be doing it in this region.

Yorkshire is famous for the quality of its produce - from cheese to herbs to meat. Less talked about is how brilliant the fish is from the North East and Hartlepool. It's truly world class and it has been fantastic to get my hands on it again.

Local provenance is important but it's not the whole story. If the farm down the road has the best quality produce then use it, but if it doesn't, then I believe a chef should go elsewhere. The relationship with ingredients suppliers and producers is vitally important but ultimately it's the chefs who are putting amazing food on plates.

In this region, there are some amazing chefs doing exactly that. The best ones are taking advantage of the unique opportunity that cooking here offers. The north's long heritage and strong sense of self gives our chefs an incredible foundation to build on and great freedom to experiment with different tastes and flavours.

This book showcases some of those talented - extremely hardworking - chefs. Enjoy their recipes and the inspiration behind them but, best of all, go and discover their restaurants, taste what they do and experience some great northern hospitality.

On my return, I realised that you don't get a welcome anywhere quite like you get in the north. I believe that when we combine that glorious hospitality with great produce, our culinary heritage and experimentation, our restaurants won't only be the best in the north but arguably some of the best in the UK.

It's great to be back.

Michael Wignall
Chef Patron, Angel Inn at Hetton

1910 STEAK & SEAFOOD

Spanish City, Spanish City Plaza, Whitley Bay, Tyne & Wear, NE26 1BG

0191 691 7090
www.spanishcity.co.uk/1910-steak-seafood Twitter: @myspanishcity
Facebook: @1910SpanishCity Instagram @1910_spanishcity

The beautiful restaurant of 1910, with stunning sea views, specialises in spectacular steak and seafood dishes served in contemporary surroundings.

Situated inside the iconic Spanish City, following a redevelopment project that saw the building restored to its former glory 18 years after its final closure, 1910 is the jewel in the crown of the venue. Named in recognition of the year Spanish City originally opened, 1910 provides a space for guests to enjoy fine dining with a twist.

Floor to ceiling windows perfectly frame the vast and stunning coastline, creating the perfect backdrop for diners. Inside, the contemporary venue is light and slick, boasting a view from every table.

The menu includes opulent and creative dishes that will tantalise your taste buds with flavours both classic and innovative. With outstanding service and use of only the best ingredients going into everything they create, 1910 is the perfect place to make memories that will last a lifetime.

With floor to ceiling windows framing a panorama of the North Sea, 1910 Steak & Seafood offers a fine dining experience like no other.

CURED SALMON, SMOKED SALMON MOUSSE, BURNT APPLE, LEMON, DILL OIL

SERVES 4

Berton Vineyard, Winemakers Reserve Viognier, 2017, New South Wales (Australia)
This alluring Viognier displays lifted aromas of nectarine and peach, complemented by floral nuances of jasmine and orange blossom. Flavours intensify on the palate with soft fleshy mandarin and marmalade fruit coming to the fore. The wine finishes with moderate length and hints of baked apple and spice.

Ingredients

Cured Salmon

300g sea salt
100g sugar
10g white peppercorns (lightly crushed)
10g coriander seeds (crushed)
1 bunch dill (chopped)
4 lemons (juice and grated zest of)
2 oranges (juice and grated zest of)
900g salmon fillet (skin on)

Smoked Salmon Mousse

200g smoked salmon (chilled)
¼ lemon (juice of)
cayenne (2 pinches of)
salt (pinch of)
300ml whipping cream
2 leaves gelatine (soaked in cold water)

Burnt Apple Purée

3 red apples (cored, chopped)
50g butter
water (splash of)
1 lemon (juice of)

Lemon Jelly

200ml lemon juice
150ml water, 180g sugar
3½ leaves gelatine (softened in cold water)

Dill Oil

½ bunch dill (washed), 125ml rapeseed oil

Garnish

1 Granny Smith apple (*julienne*)
celery leaves, dill fronds, dill powder

Method

For The Cured Salmon (Prepare ahead)

Mix the salt, sugar, peppercorns, coriander, dill, citrus juices and zests to make the marinade. Rub into the salmon fillet, then cover with cling film. Leave to marinate for 24 hours. Rinse off the marinade under cold running water, then pat the salmon dry.

> **Chef's Tips**
>
> Use the best quality salmon that you can. We use Loch Duart salmon. Always buy from your local fishmonger and support the industry. The quality will also be better.
>
> Keep any spare dill oil by pouring into ice cube trays and freezing to make sure it is perfectly preserved.

For The Smoked Salmon Mousse

Blitz the salmon in a food processor briefly until smooth. Add the lemon juice, cayenne and salt. Pulse in half the cream, then force the mix through a fine sieve into a stainless steel bowl. Chill for 10 minutes. Soften the gelatine in cold water, then melt and beat into the mousse. Lightly whip the remaining cream and fold in. Refrigerate until needed.

For The Burnt Apple Purée

Place the apples in a pan with the butter and cook on a high heat until the apples start to caramelise on the bottom of the pan. Scrape the bottom of the pan, then lower the heat and cook until the apples are tender. Add the remaining ingredients and purée until smooth. Transfer to a squeezy bottle.

For The Lemon Jelly

Simmer the lemon juice, water and sugar until dissolved. Stir in the gelatine, then pour into a container and leave to cool.

For The Dill Oil

Thoroughly dry the dill. Gently heat the oil, add the dill, then remove from the heat. Leave to infuse.

To Serve

Serve as pictured.

PAVE OF HALIBUT, COMPRESSED CUCUMBER, SHELLFISH BROTH, SEA HERBS

SERVES 4

Domaine Brigitte Cerveau, Petit Chablis Brigitte Cerveau 2012, Burgundy, Petit Chablis (France) Elegant and crisp with vibrant citrus fruits, enveloped in mineral complexity. The fresh and fruity characters are supported by a rounded and textured palate.

Ingredients

Shellfish Broth

1 carrot (diced)
1 onion (diced)
1 stick celery (diced)
½ head fennel (diced)
1 star anise
12 black peppercorns
4 parsley stalks
1 tbsp tomato purée
4 crab heads
25ml cognac
water (to cover)
4 egg whites

Compressed Cucumber

1 cucumber (peeled, skin reserved)
water (splash of)

Mussels

1 shallot (chopped)
1 clove garlic (chopped)
3 stalks parsley
150g mussels
100ml white wine

Halibut And Langoustines

4 x 80g pavés of halibut (dry brined)
8 langoustines
lemon (spritz of)
butter (knob of)

Garnish

2g sea purslane, 2g oyster leaf
4g salty fingers

Method

For The Shellfish Broth (Prepare ahead)

Sweat the *mirepoix*, star anise, peppercorns and parsley stalks with no colour until soft. Add the tomato purée and crab heads and crush with a rolling pin. *Deglaze* with the cognac and cover with water. Bring to the boil, then simmer for 6 hours skimming when necessary. Pass through a *chinois*, then through a muslin cloth and chill. Check the seasoning.

To *clarify* the broth, whisk the egg whites to soft peaks, then whisk into the chilled stock. Transfer into a pan and slowly simmer until a firm crust has formed. Make a small hole in the crust and ladle out the consommé. Reduce by one-third.

Chef's Tip

This recipe will yield 20 portions of the shellfish broth but it is easier to make in batches of this size and it freezes well.

For The Compressed Cucumber

Cut the flesh of the cucumber into rectangles, 8cm x 4cm. Place the skin and trimmings into a blender with a splash of water and blitz. Pass the juice through a fine sieve and place a spoon of the juice along with a piece of cucumber into a vac pack bag, compress. Alternatively, use uncompressed cucumber.

For The Mussels

Sweat the shallot, garlic and parsley stalks with no colour until soft. Add the mussels and white wine, then cover. When the mussels have opened, strain and reserve the stock.

To Cook The Fish And To Serve

Pan roast the halibut caramelising on one side, turn over and add a few drops of lemon juice and a knob of butter.

Add the langoustines to a hot pan and colour on one side, finish with a drop of lemon juice and butter.

Remove the cucumber from the bag and place onto the plancha (grill), scorch on one side.

Add the mussels and mussel *liquor* into a pan and warm through.

Place the halibut into the centre of the bowl with the mussels around, add the langoustine to one side. Place the cucumber on the halibut. Garnish with the sea herbs. Pour the consommé into a teapot to serve at the table.

BAKED CUSTARD, SALTED CRUMBLE, BLACKBERRY SORBET

SERVES 6

Château Suduiraut, Castelnau de Suduiraut
Sauternes 2008, Bordeaux (France)
On the nose, the wine shows intense honeycomb,
beeswax and spice; the palate is lush and
sweet with honeyed flavours giving onto a spicy,
toasty finish.

Ingredients

Baked Custard

400ml double cream
200ml whole milk
1 vanilla pod (scraped)
100g caster sugar
8 egg yolks

Salted Crumble

450g butter
300g Demerara sugar
300g plain flour
300g oats
10g baking powder
10g salt

Honeycomb

40g golden syrup
10ml water
200g sugar
2 tsp bicarbonate of soda

Blackberry Sorbet

500ml water
300g sugar
150g glucose
1 litre blackberry purée
2 lemons (juice of)

Garnish

fresh blackberries
herbs
sugar tuile

6 chef's rings (lined with cling film)
baking tray (greased)

Method

For The Baked Custard

Preheat the oven to 100°C (fan).

Bring the cream, milk, vanilla seeds and pod to the boil. Mix the sugar and egg yolks together, then pour the cream mix over and stir well. Pour into the prepared rings and bake until set, about 15-20 minutes.

Chef's Tip

Skim any bubbles from the top of the custard before baking for a smooth finish.

For The Salted Crumble

Preheat the oven to 180°C (fan).

Cream the butter and sugar together, then add the remaining ingredients. Bake until golden, about 15-20 minutes, stirring every 5 minutes.

For The Honeycomb

Bring all the ingredients, except the bicarb, to the boil and allow to become a golden caramel. Stir in the bicarb, then pour out onto a greased tray and allow to cool.

For The Blackberry Sorbet (Prepare ahead)

Gently bring all the ingredients to the boil to dissolve the sugar. Chill, then freeze and Pacotize. Alternatively, churn in an ice cream machine or freeze in a plastic container, stirring every 20 minutes.

To Serve

Serve as pictured, garnished with fresh blackberries and herbs.

026
ACKLAM HALL

Hall Drive, Acklam, Middlesbrough, TS5 7DY

01642 822 000
www.acklamhall.co.uk Twitter: @AcklamHall Facebook: Acklam Hall

A ward-winning Acklam Hall has gone from strength to strength since reopening after an extensive renovation in 2016. Middlesbrough's only Grade I listed building dates back to 1683 and, over the years, has been home to myriad of uses, from a family home to a grammar school. Now this notable establishment hosts a wedding, event and conference centre. However the main focus for the Hall has to be the food, with three private dining rooms and the restaurant serving all day.

From Acklam's afternoon teas, voted the best in Teesside by TeaReviews.co.uk in 2018, to the Brierley Dining Room, the Hall's prized asset, with its ornate ceilings and stunning décor, it's the perfect venue for a romantic dinner and fine dining experience.

Head chef Richard Greenup, recognised in the Michelin Guide, is delighted to head up the kitchen. "We like to bring great food in a fantastic setting whilst delivering friendly, professional, non-intrusive service," says Richard. Along with his senior sous chef James West, Richard and the team focus strongly on local, sustainable, homegrown produce. "We serve food that is honest, using modern French and British techniques. Classic dishes with a modern twist, in keeping with the Hall's philosophy and ethos."

Managing director Michael Jones is proud to lead the team at Acklam Hall. "Attention to detail is second to none," says Michael. "Guests can choose from the various menus; whether it's a quick bite to eat or an elegant three course dining experience, Acklam Hall is renowned as one of the most exclusive places to eat in Middlesbrough. Such stunning surroundings, with exquisite food and an extensive complementary wine list, there really is something for everyone at Acklam Hall."

Impossible as it would seem, Acklam Hall constantly strives to improve on its award-winning food.

CHARRED MACKEREL, HORSERADISH, BEETROOT

SERVES 4

Chassagne-Montrachet 1er Cru Les Macherelles 2011, Domaine Guy Amiot, Burgundy (France)

Ingredients

Beetroot Gel

500ml beetroot juice
5g agar agar
salt (pinch of)
15ml red wine vinegar

Horseradish Cream

150g horseradish sauce
250ml double cream
2 lemons (juice of)
salt (pinch of)

Beetroot

4 egg whites
300g cooking salt
6 baby beetroot

Bread Crisps

2 slices thick white bread (crusts removed)
oil (drizzle of)
salt (pinch of)

Mackerel

4 mackerel fillets
10ml rapeseed oil

To Serve

1 medium candied beetroot (thinly sliced)
micro herbs

Method

For The Beetroot Gel

Warm the beetroot juice with the agar agar, then refrigerate. Once set, blend and season with salt and red wine vinegar. Transfer to a squeezy bottle for serving.

For The Horseradish Cream

Combine the horseradish, cream, lemon juice and a pinch of salt, then pass through a sieve. Whip until stiff, then refrigerate.

For The Beetroot

Preheat the oven to 180°C (fan).

Whisk the egg whites until stiff peaks are formed, then fold through the salt. Pack the egg white mix around the beetroots to form an airtight dome. Bake for 20 minutes. Leave the beets to cool slightly, then peel with your hands and cut into wedges.

For The Bread Crisps

Preheat the oven to 160°C (fan).

Roll the bread between 2 slices of greaseproof paper, then cut into triangles. Oil and season the bread, then bake between 2 flat trays for 9 minutes.

For The Mackerel

Remove any bones and trim the fillet edges for presentation. Heat a non-stick pan and add the oil. Place the mackerel, skin-side down, on parchment and cook until the skin is crispy. Take the pan off the heat and turn the mackerel over. The residual heat will continue to cook the mackerel.

> **Chef's Tip**
>
> When cooking fish, use greaseproof paper to avoid sticking and tearing of the skin.

To Serve

Squeeze small and large dots of beetroot gel on the plate. Add the salt baked beetroots and mackerel fillet. *Quenelle* the horseradish cream and add the candied beetroot and bread crisps. Garnish with micro herbs.

DUO OF NEESHAM BEEF

SERVES 4

🍷 *Malbec Reserve 2017, Gouguenheim, Mendoza (Argentina)*

Ingredients

2 x 225g beef fillets

Beef Cheeks

2 beef cheeks
oil (drizzle of)
2 sticks celery (peeled, chopped)
2 carrots (peeled, chopped)
2 onions (peeled, chopped)
1 sprig thyme
2 cloves garlic

Onion Purée And Powder

6 onions (peeled, diced)
vegetable oil (drizzle of)
2 cloves garlic
1 sprig thyme

Jus

1 onion (peeled, diced)
1 clove garlic (crushed)
1 small sprig thyme
reserved stock from beef cheeks
1 bottle red wine

Fondant Potato

2 large potatoes
250g unsalted butter
1 sprig thyme
1 clove garlic
salt (pinch of)
water (to cover)

To Serve

4 baby carrots (boiled, then pan roasted)

Method

For The Beef Cheeks (Prepare ahead)

Preheat the oven to 110°C (fan).

Seal the beef cheeks until browned in oil, then place in a deep tray. Add the celery, carrots, onions, garlic and thyme. Cover with greaseproof paper, then foil and cook in the oven for 9 hours.

Once cool enough to handle, pick the beef cheek meat down, discarding any fat or sinew. Season and roll into tight cylinders in cling film, then refrigerate. Keep the stock as this will form the base of the jus.

For The Onion Purée And Powder (Prepare ahead)

Cook the onions in the oil with the garlic and thyme until golden. Remove one quarter of the onions and set aside. Blitz the remaining onions until smooth and season to taste.

Preheat the oven to 60°C.

Place the reserved onions on a baking tray and dehydrate overnight. When cool, blitz to a powder.

For The Jus

Sweat the onion with garlic and thyme until soft. Add the reserved beef stock and wine and slowly reduce until it coats the back of the spoon. Pass through a fine sieve into a clean pan.

For The Fondant Potato

Cut the potatoes into 2.5cm high cylinders and place in a pan with the butter, thyme, garlic, salt and enough water to cover. Cook until the water has evaporated and the potatoes have started to caramelise.

For The Beef Fillet

Cut the fillets into 4 portions. Place into a hot pan and seal for 1 minute on all sides (medium rare). Leave to rest in a warm place.

Chef's Tip

Ensure the beef fillet is at room temperature before cooking.

To Serve And Assemble

Preheat the oven to 180°C (fan).

Cut the beef cheeks into 2.5cm slices and reheat in the oven for 10 minutes. Place the fillet, cheek and potato fondant in the middle of the plate. Garnish with the onion purée and carrots. Finish with the jus and onion powder.

BAKED CINNAMON CREME BRULEE, RUM & RAISIN

SERVES 4

 DV by Château Doisy Védrines 2013, Sauternes, Bordeaux (France)

Ingredients

Crème Brûlée

500ml double cream
10g ground cinnamon
220g egg yolks
80g caster sugar
icing sugar (to dust)

Shortbread

125g butter
60g caster sugar
180g plain flour

Soaked Raisins

20 red grapes
50ml Lamb's navy rum
50g sugar

Raisin Purée

1 litre water
2 Earl Grey teabags
200g raisins

To Serve

1 tin Carnation caramel
rum and raisin ice cream

deep tray (lined with cling film)

Method

For The Crème Brûlée

Preheat the oven to 120°C (fan).

Gently warm the cream with the cinnamon. Whisk the egg yolks and sugar together, stir in the warm cream, then pour into the prepared tray. Cook in a *bain-marie* in the oven until set, about 40 minutes. When chilled, use a round cutter to make the cylinder shape and leave in the fridge.

For The Shortbread

Preheat the oven to 175°C (fan).

Rub together the butter, sugar and flour and place on a baking tray. Bake for 15 minutes.

For The Soaked Raisins

Preheat the oven to 50°C (fan).

Bake the grapes for 90 minutes. Make a syrup with the rum and sugar, then stir in the semi-dried grapes.

For The Raisin Purée

Bring the water to the boil, add the teabags and raisins and leave to soak for 1 hour. Pass through a sieve, remove the teabags, then blitz the raisins, adding enough of the cooking *liquor* to make a smooth purée.

To Assemble

Place dots of caramel and raisin purée artistically on a plate. Glaze the brûlée by dusting with icing sugar and heating with a blow torch. Crumble the shortbread and add to the plate along with the soaked raisins. Serve with a *rocher* of rum and raisin ice cream.

036
THE ANGEL AT HETTON

The Angel Inn, Hetton, Skipton, BD23 6LT

01756 730 263
www.angelhetton.co.uk Twitter: @AngelHetton

One of the original gastro-pubs, the Angel Inn at Hetton in the beautiful North Yorkshire Dales, has begun a new chapter in its long history with the arrival of Michael Wignall as chef patron. Michael and his wife Johanna took over in September 2018. Their combined vision is to keep everything that the Angel was known and loved for - a warm welcome, a deep connection with its location and fantastic food - and make it outstanding.

Two Michelin-starred chef Michael has reimagined the pub's offering and created a fabulous new menu for the 60-seat restaurant. In 2019, a brand new fine dining restaurant called Cove will be added to the mix, putting the Angel on every gourmet food lover's bucket list.

With a style that's casual and contemporary, the new Angel is all about great food and great hospitality - and it aims to give people a relaxed experience no matter who they are or where they choose to dine, Angel or Cove. With a style of cooking that combines classical training with eclectic influences, experimentation and meticulous attention to detail, Michael puts food that wows on every plate.

"I believe in taking influences from around you and then breaking with tradition because people want a wide variety of flavours to keep food interesting" says Michael.

The newly refurbished Angel is five miles north of Skipton and transport can be provided; there's also a small number of well-appointed bedrooms available to book. Open for breakfast, lunch and dinner.

With Michelin-starred chef Michael Wignall at the helm, the Angel Inn at Hetton is destined to become a must-visit destination in the North of England for all lovers of fine food and great hospitality.

YORKSHIRE DALES POULTRY PRESSING, PHEASANT LIVER PARFAIT, CELERY GEL

SERVES 25-30

 Viognier Les Vignes d'a Côte, Yves Cuilleron (France)

Ingredients

Terrine Stock
1 litre reduced brown chicken stock (boiling)
100ml dashi
10 leaves bronze gelatine (soaked in cold water)

Terrine
1 large whole chicken, 30ml olive oil
4 whole wood pigeons (head, wings, wishbone, guts removed), 5g butter, 4 rabbit saddle (*larder trimmed*), ½g tarragon

Chicken Brine
4 litres water, 225g salt, 125g sugar
1 bunch tarragon, 1 bunch parsley, 2 bay leaves
1 bulb garlic, 1 onion
30g black pepper (blitzed), 2 lemons (halved)

Pigeon Brine
106g brown sugar, 72g salt, 6.8g pink salt
7 peppercorns, ½ bunch thyme, 3 bay leaves
6 cloves, 4 cloves garlic, 2g juniper, 1 litre water

Vegetables
2 Savoy cabbages (leaves separated)
250g trompette mushrooms (cleaned, trimmed, seasoned), salt and pepper

Reduction
20ml Madeira, 20ml white port, 20ml brandy
4 peppercorns, ½ bay leaf,
1 clove garlic, 1 sprig thyme

Pheasant Liver Parfait
250g pheasant liver, 25g pink salt, 2½ eggs
250g unsalted butter (warmed), salt and pepper
50ml whipping cream

Celery Gel
200ml celery juice mixed with Ultratex until thick

To Serve
100g maple peas (cooked in 200ml barrel aged Minus 8 vinegar)
200g Muscat grapes (semi-dried)
smoking gun, 30 x 20 x 3cm terrine dish (double lined with cling film)

Method

For The Terrine Stock
Combine the ingredients, pass through fine muslin, set aside.

For The Chicken (Allow 48 hours minimum)
Simmer the chicken brine ingredients, then chill. Brine for 12 hours. Pat dry, refrigerate for 24 hours. Reserve a quarter of the brine.
Remove the legs and breast. Place the legs into a vac pack bag with 10ml of olive oil and cook *sous vide* for 12 hours at 68°C. Place the breasts in a vac pack bag with 10ml of olive oil and cook at 62°C for 1½ hours. Slice into 1cm strips.

For The Wood Pigeon (Prepare ahead)
Lightly simmer the pigeon brine ingredients with half the water for 3 minutes. Add the remaining water and cool for 8 hours. Pass through a fine sieve.
Pull the pigeon skin taught and lightly blow torch. Cool. Remove the breasts and brine in a vac pack bag for 12 hours. Refrigerate, skin-side down, on a rack for 12 hours. Smoke for 10 minutes, then vac pack and cook *sous vide* at 58°C for 12 minutes.
Pat dry, cook, skin-side down, on a medium heat with olive oil for 30 seconds. Add 5g of butter, heat until foaming, flip the breasts and cook for 10 seconds. Cool, then slice into 1cm strips.

For The Rabbit (Prepare ahead)
Steep the loins in the reserved chicken brine for 3 hours. Dry for 12 hours on a rack in the fridge. Roll the loins tightly, in clingfilm, into a sausage shape, securing at each end. Refrigerate overnight. Snip off both ends, place in a vac pack bag (in the cling film) with 10ml of oil and the tarragon. Cook *sous vide* for 18 minutes at 58°C. Cut in half lengthways.

For The Vegetables
Cook the Savoy until soft, refresh in iced water. Roll with a rolling pin, then place onto a tray with a little warm terrine stock. Lightly fry the mushrooms in oil.

To Assemble The Terrine (Prepare ahead)
Line the mould with cabbage leaves. Place the meats and mushrooms into the mould in alternating layers, seasoning and pouring a little warm terrine stock over each layer. Finish with a layer of cabbage. Cover with a double layer of cling film. Press with a weight for 6 hours. Slice carefully.

For The Pheasant Liver Parfait (Prepare ahead)
Reduce the reduction ingredients by half. Pass through a sieve and blend.
Blend the livers, salt and eggs. Add the warm reduction, butter and seasoning. Pass into a vac pack bag. Cook *sous vide* for 45 minutes at 67°C. Cool in ice for 5 hours. Remove from the bag and fold in the cream. Place into a piping bag.

To Serve
Serve as pictured.

YORKSHIRE PARTRIDGE, BOUDIN NOIR PUREE, GAME JUS

SERVES 4

Crozes-Hermitage, Domaine du Colombier, Rhône (France)

Ingredients

Partridge Brine

4 litres water
225g salt
30g white pepper
125g sugar
1 bunch tarragon
1 bunch parsley
2 bay leaves
1 bulb garlic
1 onion
2 lemons (halved)

Partridge

4 long legged partridges (feathers removed)
10ml pomace oil
2 sprigs thyme
2 sprigs rosemary

Boudin Noir Purée

50ml Cabernet Sauvignon vinegar
100ml Madeira
100ml ruby port
280ml chicken stock
4 boudin noir (peeled)

Sauce

partridge legs
50g butter
20ml olive oil
200ml game stock
1 sprig thyme
8 juniper berries (crushed)
lemon (spritz of)
salt and pepper

Garnish

barbecued Hispi cabbage
parsnip bark and purée
parsley *emulsion*
boudin crumb

Method

For The Partridge Brine (Prepare ahead)

Bring half the water to the boil and mix in the salt and pepper. Add the aromats, sugar and remaining water and leave for about 20 minutes (you must be able to taste the aromats). Chill.

To Prepare The Partridge (Prepare ahead)

Check the bird for shot, then remove the wings and head but leave the neck. Pick the bird up by the neck and lightly thrust downwards, this loosens the joints and makes it easier to work with. Remove the legs, being careful to leave as much skin on the crown as possible. Set the legs aside. Flip the bird over, make a small incision in the back of the neck and cut upwards. Turn back over and pull the skin gently over the breast. Remove the crop sack in one piece and any excess fat. Scrape along the back of the wishbone to free in one piece and remove. Remember not to cut into the breasts. Remove the neck and pull the skin back over the bird. Lightly blow torch and add to the chilled brine for 12 hours.

> **Chef's Tip**
>
> We lightly brine our partridges on the crown and allow to dry for 2 days. The care taken in the preparation really shows on the final product.

For The Partridge

Vac pack each partridge with the pomace oil, thyme and rosemary. *Sous vide* at 58°C for 45 minutes, then pan fry to colour. Leave to rest for a few minutes before serving.

For The Boudin Noir Purée

Reduce the vinegar by half, add the alcohols and reduce to a syrup. Add the stock and bring to the boil.

Cook the boudin noir in a separate pan, then transfer to a powerful blender. Add enough of the liquid to achieve your desired purée consistency.

For The Sauce

Chop the partridge legs into small pieces. Heat the butter and oil until foaming, then add the legs. Cook until golden brown, then remove. Clean the pan with a paper towel to remove any excess oil and place the browned legs back into the pan. *Deglaze* with the stock. Reduce the mixture and bring to a light simmer, consistently skimming. Add the thyme and simmer for 1½ hours. Stir in the juniper berries, then pass through a fine cloth, blend with a small amount of butter and a squeeze of lemon. Season to taste.

To Serve

Serve as pictured.

'SNICKERS'- PEANUT PARFAIT, SALTED CARAMEL, CHOCOLATE, MILK

SERVES 20

 Skillogalee Liqueur Muscat
(Australia)

Ingredients

Peanut Praline

300g caster sugar, 100ml water
500g peanuts (roasted until golden)

Praline Parfait

1kg mascarpone
700ml whipping cream
275g egg yolks
300g caster sugar
100ml water
20g leaf gelatine (soaked in iced water)
200g peanut praline

Chocolate Rocks

300g dark chocolate (70%, melted)
2½g salt, 75g Sosa Maltosec

Chocolate Gel

340g blonde chocolate (melted)
200ml milk, 10g glucose
7½g leaf gelatine (soaked in iced water)
400ml UHT whipping cream

Salted Caramel

550g sugar, water (as required)
360ml double cream
1 vanilla pod (scraped)
240g butter (diced), vanilla salt

Milk Ice Cream

500g peanuts (roasted until dark), 100g sugar
25g milk powder, 10g glucose powder
5g Stabb 2000 stabiliser
1.1 litre whole milk
2g leaf gelatine (soaked in iced water)

Set Custard

1 litre UHT whipping cream
1 vanilla pod (scraped)
80g caster sugar (mixed with 4½g of Pectin X58)
240g pasteurised yolks

Method

For The Peanut Praline
Mix the sugar with the water and heat to a caramel. Add the nuts and blend the caramel mixture for 5 minutes until hot. Cool, then blend again. Repeat this process until liquid, 20 minutes. Pass through a sieve. Set aside.

For The Praline Parfait (Prepare ahead)
Mix the mascarpone with 200ml of the cream. Semi-whip the remaining cream and refrigerate. Whisk the yolks in a KitchenAid for 8 minutes. Whilst whisking, mix the sugar and water to a paste and heat to 118°C. Turn the eggs down to the lowest speed and slowly pour in the sugar mixture, then increase speed to medium. Squeeze the gelatine and melt in a small saucepan. Add the warm gelatine to the mix, then the peanut praline. Gently whisk half the mascarpone mix into the egg mixture. Add the other half and turn the speed up again. Transfer to a large mixing bowl, fold in the remaining whipped cream. Pipe into desired mould, freeze for 12 hours.

For The Chocolate Rocks (Prepare ahead)
Combine the ingredients, knead by hand (with gloves on), then gently pull apart. Set aside for 24 hours.

For The Chocolate Gel (Prepare ahead)
Warm the milk and glucose, then add the gelatine. Pass through a sieve into the chocolate and *emulsify*. Add the cream, cover in cling film and refrigerate for 12 hours.

For The Salted Caramel
Mix the sugar and water to a paste, heat over a medium heat and take to a dark caramel until it starts to smoke.
Warm the cream with the vanilla. Remove the caramel from the heat, add the cream, then slowly add the butter. Add salt to taste. Pass through a sieve and set aside.

For The Milk Ice Cream (Prepare ahead)
Mix the dry ingredients together. Heat the milk to 35°C, add the dry ingredients and continue to heat to 90°C. Remove from the heat and add the gelatine. Stir in the nuts and refrigerate overnight. Pass through a sieve then place in a Pacojet. Alternatively, churn in an ice cream machine.

For The Set Custard (Prepare ahead)
Heat the cream and vanilla in a pan to 35°C, then add the sugar. Boil for 1 minute. Pour a little over the yolks to *temper*, then combine fully. Heat in the pan for 10 seconds, then pass through a sieve. Set overnight.

To Serve
Serve as pictured.

046
BROCKLEY HALL BOUTIQUE HOTEL & RESTAURANT

Glenside, Saltburn-by-the-Sea, TS12 1JS

01287 622 179
www.brockleyhallhotel.com Twitter: @HallBrockley Facebook: Brockley Hall Hotel

Brockley Hall Boutique Hotel and Restaurant is situated in the beautiful town of Saltburn-by-the-Sea, which has been recognised as one of the top 10 places to live in Britain.

Saltburn is famous for its pier, water powered funicular cliff lift and Victorian pleasure gardens, as well as its vibrant arts scene and huge variety of eating places celebrated in the annual food festival.

Brockley Hall is a beautiful Victorian building which has been restored in an individual and quirky style with a range of double, twin and family rooms and individually designed suites with freestanding feature baths, perfect for romantic breaks.

The hotel has a spectacular restaurant in which to enjoy the award-winning fine dining menu, as well as serving well known favourites from their á la carte menu. The delightful hand-painted conservatory and sumptuous lounge are ideal for sampling the lunch menu or handcrafted afternoon teas.

The restaurant was awarded 2 AA Rosettes in the first year of opening for its fine dining menu.

The head chef, Scott Miller, and his team of talented and inventive chefs will take you on a journey of taste with unique menus which make the most of fabulous, locally sourced ingredients. Brockley Hall is working with some of the UK's best wine merchants to provide a unique wine list to complement this most exciting of dining experiences.

Modern British food delivering a gastronomic journey through each course. Brockley Hall was awarded 2 AA Rosettes within the first year of opening, something they are undoubtedly proud of.

RABBIT BALLOTINE, HERITAGE CARROTS, CAPERS, RAISINS, SHERRY VINEGAR

SERVES 4

 Fleurie 'Vieilles Vignes' Domaine Lardy, Beaujolais, Loire, 2015 (France)

Ingredients

Rabbit Ballotine

1 chicken breast (diced), 20g chervil
100ml double cream, salt (to season)
1 rabbit (skinned, gutted, fillets removed, legs and carcass reserved)
3 slices Parma ham

Confit Rabbit Leg Balls

2 rabbit legs, 100g duck fat
100ml reduced rabbit stock
1 leaf bronze gelatine (soaked in cold water)
10g flat leaf parsley (finely chopped)
salt (to season)
sherry vinaigrette (splash of)
plain flour, beaten egg, breadcrumbs (to *pane*)

Pickled Heritage Carrots

3 purple baby carrots (peeled)
3 yellow baby carrots (peeled)
200ml white wine vinegar
200ml water, 20g sugar, 6 coriander seeds
2 star anise, 100ml rapeseed oil, 3g salt

Sherry Vinegar Jelly

50ml sherry vinegar
150ml water, 20g caster sugar
2g salt, 2g agar agar

Raisin And Caper Purée

100g raisins, 20g capers
100ml white wine
water (to cover)
salt and sugar (to season)
½ lemon (juice of)

Chervil Crème Fraîche

(Combine the ingredients in a bowl)
50g crème fraîche, 8g chervil (finely chopped)

Garnish

pomme soufflés, nasturtium leaves

Method

For The Rabbit Ballotine (Prepare ahead)
Pulse the chicken breast in a blender to a paste, add the chervil and cream and pulse until smooth. Season well. Pass the mix through a drum sieve and transfer to a piping bag. Place the Parma ham, slightly overlapping, on top of some cling film. Lay the rabbit loins side by side across the length of the Parma ham. Pipe a line of mousse along the ridge in the middle of the loins. Roll into a ballotine and tie off each end. Cook at 72°C in a water bath for 45 minutes, then plunge into iced water to chill. Alternatively, roast in the oven for 30 minutes (180°C).

For The Confit Rabbit Leg Balls (Prepare ahead)
Place the legs and duck fat in a vac pack bag, seal and cook at 86°C for 10 hours. Alternatively, *confit* in the oven (120°C) for 4 hours or until fork tender.
Remove from the bag and drain off the duck fat. When cool, carefully pick the meat off the bones. Warm the rabbit stock, whisk in the gelatine, then pass through a sieve onto the rabbit meat. Don't add all the liquid in one go; you want the mix to be moist, not wet.
Add the parsley, salt and vinaigrette. Roll the leg mix into 20g balls and freeze until hard. When ready to serve, *pane* the balls and deep fry at 180°C until golden.

> **Chef's Tip**
> Freezing the rabbit leg balls will allow you to *pane* them more easily without them breaking up.

For The Pickled Heritage Carrots
Bring all ingredients, apart from the carrots, to a simmer until the sugar has dissolved. Split the *liquor* into 2 pans, then bring to the boil. Add the carrots to the separate pans, boil for 1 minute, cover the pans with cling film, then set aside and leave to cool.

For The Sherry Vinegar Jelly (Prepare ahead)
Bring all the ingredients, except the agar agar, to the boil, then whisk in the agar agar and boil for 3 minutes. Pour into a cling film lined tray to around 4mm thick. Chill for 3 hours, then cut into squares.

For The Raisin And Caper Purée
Place the raisins, capers and wine in a pan and cover with cold water. Bring to the boil, then simmer for 15 minutes. Drain the liquid and reserve. Blend the capers and raisins with some of the *liquor* to make a smooth, thick paste. Season with sugar, lemon juice and salt (if required). Pass through a sieve.

To Serve
Assembled as pictured.

NORTH ATLANTIC COD, LANGOUSTINE, CROSNES, RAINBOW KALE, SMOKED COD ROE EMULSION

SERVES 4

🍷 *O Rosal, Bodegas Terras Gauda, Rias Baixas, 2016 (Spain)*

Ingredients

Smoked Cod Roe Emulsion

100g smoked cod roe
20g pasteurised egg yolk
80ml water
200ml vegetable oil
lemon juice and salt (to season)

Samphire Powder

200g samphire
salt and sugar (to taste)

Crispy Rainbow Kale

200g rainbow kale
vegetable oil (to deep fry)
salt (to season)

Cod, Crosnes And Langoustines

4 x 120g cod loin portions
30g butter
crosnes (handful of)
2 raw langoustines (shelled)
½ lemon (juice of)

Garnish

frisée lettuce

Method

For The Smoked Cod Roe Emulsion (Prepare ahead)

Place the roe, yolk and water into a blender and blend until smooth. Slowly add the oil to create a thick mayonnaise consistency. Season to taste with salt and lemon juice, then pass through a sieve and chill.

For The Samphire Powder (Prepare the day before)

Dehydrate the samphire in a dehydrator or a very low oven for 24 hours at 60°C or until completely dry, then blend and season to taste. Pass through a fine sieve to create a dust.

For The Crispy Rainbow Kale

Remove the stalks from the centre of the kale leaves. Deep fry the leaves in oil (180°C) for around 1 minute. Remove from the oil, season and leave in a warm place to go crisp.

> **Chef's Tip**
> We use 3 different types of kale to mix this recipe up a bit. Use the freshest you can find.

For The Cod, Crosnes And Langoustines

Place the cod, skin-side down, in a cold, oiled pan over a medium to high heat and cook until you have a golden, crisp skin. Remove the pan from the heat and add the butter, moving the pan constantly so as not to burn the butter. Once foaming, add the crosnes and keep basting the butter over the crosnes and cod. Return the pan to the heat and, when the cod is nearly cooked, add the langoustines. Once cooked through, spritz the pan with lemon and place everything onto a cloth before assembling.

To Serve

Serve as pictured and garnish with frisée lettuce.

BROCKLEY HALL'S OWN LEMON TOP, LEMONADE PARFAIT, BUCKWHEAT TUILE

SERVES 4-6

Petit Manseng Doux, Cuvée Gaston Phoebus,
Cabidos, 2011 (South West of France)

Ingredients

Vanilla And Lemonade Parfait

180g pasteurised egg white
250g caster sugar
350ml double cream
100ml whole milk
1 vanilla pod (scraped)
lemonade flavouring
liquid yellow food colouring
1 tbsp crackle crystals

Tuile Cones

50g egg white
50g icing sugar
50g butter (melted, cooled)
50g plain flour

Lemon Curd

3 medium eggs
70g caster sugar
100ml lemon juice
125g butter (diced)

Buckwheat Tuile

100g fondant
50g glucose
50g isomalt
30g buckwheat grains (toasted, blitzed)

Lemon Sorbet Topping

250ml sugar stock syrup
125ml cold water
4 lemons (zest and juice of)
0.1g citric acid
0.1g malic acid
yellow food colouring

To Serve

vanilla ice cream, candy floss

4 cone moulds
22cm x 15cm tray (for the parfait)

Method

For The Vanilla And Lemonade Parfait (Prepare ahead)

Place the egg white and sugar in a bowl and whisk over a *bain-marie* until light and fluffy (Swiss meringue), then remove from the *bain-marie* and whisk in a machine until cool.

Whisk the cream and milk to soft peaks. Gently fold the cream mix into the meringue, then divide into 2 equal amounts.

Flavour half the mix with the vanilla seeds. Spread evenly in a tray lined with cling film and freeze until firm enough to add the next layer.

Mix the lemonade flavouring, colouring and crackle crystals into the remaining mix. Spread evenly over the vanilla parfait and return to the freezer to set.

For The Tuile Cones

Mix the egg white and icing sugar in a bowl, slowly add the liquid butter. Stir in the flour until a smooth paste forms, then refrigerate.

Preheat the oven to 160°C (fan).

Spread the mix over a non-stick baking sheet in triangle shapes. Bake for 8-10 minutes until the edges turn golden. Remove from the oven and, while still warm, wrap around a cone mould. Cool.

For The Lemon Curd (Prepare ahead)

Place the eggs, sugar and lemon juice in a Thermomix set on 100°C, speed 4, for 10 minutes. Add the butter until fully incorporated, then pass through a sieve. Alternatively, whisk continuously over a *bain-marie* until the mix reaches 90°C and is at the ribbon stage. Refrigerate.

For The Buckwheat Tuile (Prepare ahead)

Slowly melt the fondant, glucose and isomalt in a heavy-based pan. Once dissolved, raise the temperature until a light caramel is achieved. Stir the blitzed buckwheat into the caramel. Pour into a tray. Cool.

Preheat the oven to 160°C (fan).

Blitz the set caramel to a powder, dust over a tray and bake until the sugar melts again. Allow to cool slightly, then cut into rectangles the same height as the parfait.

For The Lemon Sorbet Topping (Prepare ahead)

Combine all the ingredients, except the colouring. Pass through a sieve, then add the colouring until very yellow - the mix will lighten whilst being churned. It will taste sharp but the flavour will mellow when frozen. Churn in an ice cream machine to a piping consistency. Freeze.

To Assemble

Fill each cone with vanilla ice cream. Top with the lemon sorbet topping and arrange as pictured.

THE BRUCE ARMS

Main Street, West Tanfield, Ripon, North Yorkshire, HG4 5JJ

01677 470 325
www.thebrucearms.com Twitter: @thebrucearms

The Bruce Arms, in the centre of the historic village of West Tanfield, is an18th Century coaching inn which served the route through Wensleydale, 'over the top' to Kendal in the Lake District.

The horse-drawn coaches may be long gone but the stable yard and walls of the old inn are steeped in the character of that bygone era. It was sketched by JMW Turner and the interior of the bar pays homage to the great artist.

The chef team, led by Dave Mathews, takes great pride in producing dishes which reflect the inn's Yorkshire heritage as well as being very contemporary. Dave is a classically trained chef and has had experience in some of the best restaurants, both in the North of England and internationally. As well as catering for formal banquet dining, the team also offers sandwiches and salads as lighter options. Seafood and steaks are extremely popular both at lunch and in the evening. Little wonder that The Bruce won Restaurant of the Year 2018 in the Flavours of Herriot Country Awards.

The Bruce is very much a family affair with Dave's wife and daughter front of house and other members of the service team declaring that they feel as if they are adopted!

Both The Bruce Arms and its sister pub, The Bull Inn, are run by Gil Richardson, another member of the family. The Bull Inn, also in the same village, is a traditional local offering a hearty pub menu. Both establishments offer bed and breakfast and share the same hallmarks of quality which make West Tanfield an ideal location for a foodie short break.

West Tanfield really does offer the best in Yorkshire hospitality. Both The Bruce Arms and The Bull Inn are award-winning establishments with recognition from Welcome to Yorkshire, Flavours of Herriot Country and Visit England.

SAUTEED TIGER PRAWNS & SQUID WITH LEMON, HERBS, TOMATO & GARLIC BUTTER SAUCE, PARMESAN TUILE

SERVES 4

 Ugni Blanc Colombard, Le Sanglier de la Montagne, Vin de Pays de l'Aude, (France) From high up in the mountains, old vines produce low yields of concentrated fruit. Aromatic and quite zesty, this wine is full of character with a wonderful zing of freshness on the finish.

Ingredients

Parmesan Tuile

200g Parmesan (finely grated)
salt and cracked black pepper

Squid And Tiger Prawns

2 squid tubes
1 tbsp cooking oil
24 tiger tail prawns (peeled)
1 bunch dill (finely chopped)
1 bunch chives (finely chopped)
10 sprigs flat leaf parsley (finely chopped)
4 plum tomatoes (finely diced, seeds in)
3 cloves garlic (crushed)
250g unsalted butter (cubed)
1 lemon (juice of)
1 tsp each of sea salt and freshly ground
black pepper

Garnish

micro salad

baking tray (lined with silicone paper)

Method

For The Parmesan Tuile

Preheat the oven to 180°C.

Using a pastry cutter as a template, sprinkle the Parmesan within the circle of the cutter onto the baking tray. Make 4 discs, leaving 2-3cm between them on the tray. Lightly season with salt and cracked black pepper. Bake in the oven for 3-4 minutes until lightly golden. Remove from the oven, allow to cool, then transfer to a wire rack using a spatula.

For The Squid And Tiger Prawns

Top and tail the squid tubes, removing 5mm from each end and discard.

Lay the tubes flat and, by running a sharp knife inside, and against the inner edge of each tube, cut through so they can be opened into one large sheet. Cut down the centre of the sheets so that you have 4 smaller sheets and dry with a paper towel. Score the flat sheets diagonally, 5mm apart and repeat in the opposite direction. Be careful not to fully cut through the squid. Cut each scored sheet into 5 or 6 triangles.

Heat the oil in a large frying pan on full heat until smoking hot. Carefully add the prawns and *sauté* for 30-40 seconds. Push the prawns to one side of the pan and add the squid. Keep the squid still in the pan for 20 seconds to allow a light scorching, then toss together.

Add the herbs, tomatoes and garlic. Stir, then add the butter and season with lemon juice, salt and pepper.

Chef's Tip

Ask your fishmonger to clean the squid. Alternatively buy frozen, prepared squid tubes and defrost them overnight in the fridge. Be careful not to overcook the squid.

To Serve

Serve immediately with the Parmesan tuile, garnished with micro salad.

CRISPY BREAST OF WEST TANFIELD LAMB, CREAMY CHIVE MASH, WILTED BRASSICAS, BABY CARROTS, RED WINE & PORT JUS

SERVES 4

Shiraz, Cranswick Estate, Barossa Valley (Australia)
The Rhone valley's most famous grape does
particularly well in Australia. Spice, black fruits and
a dusting of pepper are all found in this rich wine.

Ingredients

Lamb

2 large lamb breasts
1 tbsp sea salt
1 tbsp cracked black pepper
1 bulb garlic (crushed or puréed)
10 sprigs rosemary (4 finely chopped)
4 large carrots (diced)
1 large onion (diced)
6 cloves garlic (crushed)
250ml red wine
1 litre chicken stock

Red Wine And Port Jus

cooking *liquor* from the lamb
2 carrots (chopped)
1 large onion (chopped)
2 cloves garlic (chopped)
1 bay leaf
1 sprig rosemary, 1 sprig thyme
2 tbsp redcurrant jelly
200ml port, ½ bottle red wine

Chive Mash

4-5 large red skin potatoes (peeled, quartered)
200g salted butter (cubed)
1 tsp ground white pepper
1 bunch chives (finely chopped)

Wilted Brassicas

¼ Savoy cabbage (finely sliced)
5-6 curly kale leaves (stalks and centre
vein removed)
50g butter
nutmeg (pinch of)
salt and pepper

Method

For The Lamb

Preheat the oven to 180°C.

Lay out the lamb breast, skin-side up and, using a sharp knife, gently peel back and discard the skin. Trim fat from the lamb and discard. Turn the lamb over, then overlap the sheets to create one large square. Season with salt and pepper, spread the garlic purée over evenly, then sprinkle with the chopped rosemary. Roll the lamb as tightly as possible into a barrel shape. Cut butchers' string into 15cm lengths and tie the barrel with string, 2-3cm apart.

Place the carrots, onion, crushed garlic and rosemary sprigs in a roasting tin, then sit the lamb on top and cover with the red wine and stock. Cover with parchment paper and, with a double thickness of foil, make as tight a seal as possible. Braise for 3½ hours. Remove from the cooking *liquor* and cool. Cut the breast into 8 slices.

For The Red Wine And Port Jus

Drain the cooking *liquor* from the lamb and reduce by half. Brown the carrots, onions and garlic, then add the herbs, redcurrant jelly, red wine, port and reduced *liquor* and reduce by half again. Strain through a fine sieve.

For The Chive Mash

Cover the potatoes with water in a large pan, add a pinch of salt and boil until tender. Drain, then mash with the butter and white pepper. Stir in the chives, cover with a lid or foil and keep warm.

For The Wilted Brassicas

Wash and drain the brassicas. Melt the butter in a pan with the nutmeg, add the brassicas and toss over the heat until wilted. Season, drain and keep warm.

To Serve

Heat a frying pan, add a little oil and a knob of butter and cook the lamb until beautifully crisp on both sides. Place the mash in the centre of warm bowls or plates, using a ring for a neat finish. Top with wilted brassicas and lamb. Pour a little red wine sauce over the lamb and create a puddle around the mash.

Chef's Tip

Ask your butcher to skin and trim the fat from the lamb. It can be braised a day in advance and chilled overnight, string removed and sliced for best results.

PASSION FRUIT CHEESECAKE WITH GRANOLA BASE & PASSION FRUIT JELLY TOP

SERVES 4

*Coteaux du Layon, Domaine des Forges, Loire
Valley (France)
A light, fresh dessert wine showing a complex and
honeyed nose giving way to fresh pineapple taste.*

J.M.W. TURNER RA
Sketched in West Tanfield, 1816 on his Tour of Yorkshire

Ingredients

Passion Fruit Cheesecake Filling

250g cream cheese
250ml double cream
250ml passion fruit coulis
50g caster sugar
2½ leaves gelatine (soaked in cold water)

Granola Base

100g granola
100g digestive biscuits
1 tbsp honey
50g butter
cinnamon (pinch of)

Passion Fruit Jelly Top

250ml lemonade
1½ leaves gelatine (soaked in cold water)
4 passion fruit

To Serve

spun sugar
2 passion fruit

4 individual ring moulds

Method

For The Passion Fruit Cheesecake Filling

Mix together the cream cheese and cream in a bowl.

Gently heat the passion fruit coulis and sugar, then add the softened gelatine. Add the cream cheese mixture and beat until smooth. Set aside.

For The Granola Base

Place all the ingredients into a food processor and blend to a sandy texture.

For The Passion Fruit Jelly Top

Gently heat the lemonade, add the scooped-out centres of the passion fruit, then dissolve the gelatine in the mixture. Set aside.

To Assemble

Cover the bottom of each ring mould with the granola mixture and press into a firm layer, approximately 1cm deep. Spoon or pipe the filling on top of the base mixture, leaving 1cm at the top of the mould. Gently tap the moulds to shake down the cheesecake mixture. Refrigerate for 30 minutes, then gently strain the jelly onto the top of each dessert. Refrigerate for 4-6 hours.

To Serve

Release the cheesecakes from the metal moulds by quickly heating the sides with a blow torch. Place on the plate and garnish with half a passion fruit and spun sugar.

> **Chef's Tip**
>
> For best results, refrigerate overnight. Avoid overheating the moulds!

066
CAFÉ LILLI

83 Norton High Street, Norton, TS20 1AE

01642 554 422
www.lillicafe.co.uk Twitter: cafelilli Facebook: Cafelilli Instagram: cafelilli10

Owner Roberto Pittalis was born on the beautiful Island of Sardinia, in the city of Sassari, where his love of good food and fine wine started at a very early age. He used to help his grandparents on their farm picking the fresh produce and milking the cows. Back then, his grandparents used to make sausages, olive oil, cheese and wine and sell them in the weekly village market. Roberto's passion for fresh, local food took him all around the island and also to the mainland of Italy, working in different locations and gaining vast experience.

After gaining his catering degree in food management and sommelier, Roberto moved to England in 1992 and started working in Imperial Express in Darlington. He was co-owner of Sassari in Durham City as well as Middlesbrough and 12 years ago opened Café Lilli in Norton, which created the path for good food in this gem of a village.

"Helped by my wife Patricia and a great team of staff, I believe Café Lilli gives creative cooking and a lively atmosphere in an intimate, bistro-vibe café," says Roberto. "The team has vast experience of different culinary cultures. They are very passionate and innovative about food and our aim is to provide each guest with a memorable experience by only using the best quality, locally produced products to give a range of flavours to suit all tastes."

Cafe Lilli is made up of a young, passionate and talented team; they pride themselves on excellent knowledge and service, whilst supporting local producers. They were recently featured in the Good Food Guide 2019 for the third consecutive year.

BEETROOT, PICKLED SHALLOTS, HORSERADISH JELLY, PINK GNOCCHI, GOAT'S CHEESE SNOW

SERVES 4

🍷 *Ribolla Gialla delle Venezie, Antonutti, IGT (Italy)*

Ingredients

Pickling Liquor

120ml white wine vinegar
240ml water
90g caster sugar
1 tsp mustard seeds

Pickled Beetroot And Shallots

150g beetroot (chopped)
50g banana shallot (sliced)
200ml pickle liquid

Horseradish Jelly

80ml water
20g horseradish (finely grated)
1 leaf gelatine (soaked in cold water)

Goat's Cheese Snow

200ml water
500g goat's cheese
50ml lemon juice
salt and pepper (to season)
2 leaves gelatine (soaked in cold water)

Pink Gnocchi

1kg beetroot (peeled)
100g red skinned potatoes (peeled)
100g large potatoes (peeled)
1 egg yolk
120g 00 flour
salt and black pepper

Garnish

mint leaves
edible flowers

Method

For The Pickling Liquor

Combine all the ingredients and bring to the boil.

For The Pickled Beetroot And Shallots

Cook half the beetroot until soft, then blitz to a smooth purée.

Gently boil the remaining beetroot until *al dente*. Place in the warm pickling *liquor* along with the shallots.

For The Horseradish Jelly

Heat up the water with the horseradish, then stir in the softened gelatine. Leave to cool.

For The Goat's Cheese Snow

Warm the water and set aside. Place the goat's cheese, lemon juice and seasoning in a food processor. Stir the gelatine into the warm water, then add to the goat's cheese mix whilst blending. Place on a cool tray and break apart, leave to cool.

For The Pink Gnocchi

Place the beetroot in a blender and blitz to a purée. Pass through a fine sieve, then transfer to a saucepan. Reduce the beetroot juice by half, skimming any skin that forms on the surface. Pass the reduction through a fine sieve, then leave to cool.

Boil the potatoes in salted water for 30 minutes, or until cooked through. Pass the potatoes through a sieve and place in a mixing bowl. Fold in the egg, flour, salt and pepper and 40ml of the beetroot reduction until combined. Mould into desired shape.

Place in a pan of boiling water until the gnocchi start to float, indicating that it is cooked.

> **Chef's Tip**
>
> Boiled potatoes are perfectly fine to make gnocchi, however baking them creates a drier texture for a fluffier gnocchi.

To Serve

Serve as pictured.

PAN FRIED COD, POLENTA MOUSSE, MALAYSIAN CHILLI SAUCE

SERVES 4

Gewürztraminer Alto Adige, Walch
(Italy)

Ingredients

Polenta Mousse

100ml water
50g polenta flour
75ml whole milk
25ml double cream
25g butter (diced)
seasoning

Malaysian Chilli Sauce

2 tsp chilli sauce
2 tsp chopped garlic
2 tsp soy sauce
2 tsp sugar
2 tsp rice vinegar
2 tsp rapeseed oil

Cod

4 x 180g cod fillets (skin on)
oil (drizzle of)
salt and pepper (to season)

Garnish

3 plum tomatoes (deseeded, cut into quarters)

Method

For The Polenta Mousse

Bring the water to the boil, add the polenta and milk and stir until the mixture begins to thicken. Slowly add the cream and butter and mix until smooth. Leave to cool.

For The Malaysian Chilli Sauce

Place all the ingredients in a pan and simmer until reduced. Serve warm.

For The Cod

Rub a little oil on the skin of the cod fillets. Add, skin-side down, to a hot pan and fry the cod until almost cooked through. Flip the fillets over, then remove from the heat.

> **Chef's Tip**
> Oil and cook the cod 90% skin-side down to ensure a crispy skin.

To Serve

Quenelle the mousse on top of the cod and serve as pictured.

SALTED CARAMEL FONDANT

SERVES 4

🍷 *Vin Santo, Rocco delle Macie*
(Italy)

Ingredients

Salted Caramel Sauce

50g caster sugar
25ml double cream
salt (pinch of)

Salted Caramel Fondant

150g dark chocolate (70%), (chopped)
100g unsalted butter (softened)
2 large eggs
2 large egg yolks
35g caster sugar
35g plain flour (sifted)
4 tbsp salted caramel sauce

Caramelised Bananas

1 banana
sugar (to sprinkle)

To Serve

vanilla or toffee ice cream
flaked almonds (toasted)
micro herbs
biscuit crumb

4 dariole moulds or ramekins (buttered
and dusted with brown sugar)

Method

For The Salted Caramel Sauce

Melt down the sugar in pan on a low heat. Once it turns golden brown, slowly mix in the cream, then add salt to taste.

For The Salted Caramel Fondant

Preheat the oven to 160°C (fan).

Melt the chocolate and butter together over a *bain-marie* until combined. Set aside to cool.

Cream the whole eggs, yolks and sugar until fluffy. Mix in the chocolate mixture, then fold in the sifted flour.

Fill the moulds a quarter of the way, spoon in the caramel sauce, then half fill with more mixture. Place on a baking tray and bake for 10-12 minutes until the puddings have risen and are set on top.

Chef's Tip

Butter the moulds well to prevent the puddings from sticking and serve straight away.

For The Caramelised Bananas

Sprinkle the banana with sugar, then heat with a blow torch.

To Serve

Serve the fondants with vanilla or toffee ice cream and caramelised bananas. Garnish with toasted almond flakes, micro herbs and biscuit crumb.

076
COLMANS SEAFOOD TEMPLE

Sea Road, South Shields, NE33 2LD

0191 511 1349
www.colmansseafoodtemple.co.uk Twitter: @ColmansTemple Instagram: @colmansseafoodtemple

Colmans Seafood Temple offers an exciting family seafood restaurant, serving fantastic local seafood and coastal cuisine. It also hosts a cocktail and oyster bar, and a fish and chip and seafood takeaway. Seafood at its finest, from the land and sea to the plate; delicious, nutritious and totally natural from local suppliers.

Situated on South Shields seafront, panoramic windows offer unrivalled views of the fantastic coastline! At Colmans, they prepare original and delicious seafood dishes which are cooked to order. Relax and enjoy their simple but effective approach to seafood, whilst absorbing the vibrant atmosphere of the stunning blue flag beach. There is something for everyone at Colmans Seafood Temple. They offer a warm welcome to all and invite you enjoy some great seafood and happy times.

EST. 1926

COLMANS
Seafood Temple

CTION

Colmans Seafood Temple serves the finest coastal cuisine; striving to use local and seasonal produce wherever possible. They have sustainability and responsible sourcing methods at the heart of their ethos.

SMOKED MACKEREL PATE

SERVES 4

 Picpoul de Pinet (France) - to cut through the smokiness and richness of the pâté!

Ingredients

Smoked Mackerel Pâté

2 smoked mackerel fillets
100g cream cheese
1 tsp creamed horseradish
1 tsp Dijon mustard
½ lemon (juice and zest of)
cayenne pepper (pinch of)
black pepper (pinch of)

Pickled Cucumber

¼ cucumber
100g caster sugar
100ml water
100ml white wine vinegar
1 sprig dill (chopped)

To Serve

watercress
red onion (finely sliced)
dill
sourdough bread (toasted)

Method

For The Smoked Mackerel Pâté

Remove the skin and any pin bones from the mackerel fillets. Flake the fish into a bowl, add all the remaining ingredients and mix thoroughly. Spoon into dishes and set aside in the refrigerator.

For The Pickled Cucumber

Thinly slice the cucumber and place in a non-reactive bowl.

Bring the sugar, water and vinegar to the boil in a saucepan, then simmer gently for 5 minutes. Leave to cool slightly, then pour over the cucumber slices. When chilled, add the chopped dill.

Chef's Tip

The pickle can be used for a variety of vegetables for later use and can be stored in a sterilised glass jar or Kilner jar.

To Serve

Place the mackerel pâté on a serving dish, pile a little pickled cucumber on top and add the watercress, red onion and dill. Serve with toasted sourdough bread.

PAN ROAST HAKE, GARLIC PRAWNS, BRAISED CHORIZO IN RED WINE

SERVES 4

Pinot Noir - with the bolder flavours of the chorizo and the paprika, a Pinot Noir would be great to complement!

Ingredients

Pan Roast Hake

4 x 160g hake supremes
seasoned flour (to dust)
oil (drizzle of)
butter (knob of)
lemon (spritz of)

Red Wine Braised Chorizo

200g chorizo (2½cm cubed)
oil (drizzle of)
½ onion (finely diced)
½ fennel bulb (finely diced)
1 bay leaf
½ bottle red wine
1 star anise
1 litre veal jus

Garlic Prawns

12 king prawns (deveined)
oil (drizzle of)
sea salt (pinch of)
1 tbsp garlic butter
chopped parsley (pinch of)
lemon juice (squeeze of)

Paprika Potatoes

12 new potatoes (boiled, halved)
oil (drizzle of)
smoked paprika (to season)
sea salt (to season)
butter (knob of)

Garnish

samphire
micro herbs

Method

For The Pan Roast Hake

Preheat the oven to 180°C.

Place a little oil in a frying pan and pass the fish through seasoned flour. Fry the fish, skin-side down, until crisp and golden brown. Add a little butter, then place in the oven for 4 minutes. Remove from the oven and squeeze with lemon juice.

For The Red Wine Braised Chorizo

Fry the chorizo in a drizzle of oil in a pan until it starts to colour. Add the onion, fennel and bay leaf and cook until soft. Pour in the red wine, add the star anise and reduce by two-thirds. Add the veal jus and simmer gently until the chorizo is tender. Remove the chorizo and place in a clean pan. Pass the sauce through a fine sieve into the chorizo.

> **Chef's Tip**
>
> No need to use a great quality red wine, keep that for drinking! Add a little honey to the braised chorizo to sweeten the sauce.

For The Garlic Prawns

Heat a little oil in a non-stick pan. Season the prawns with salt, then add to the pan. Colour on both sides, then add the garlic butter. Cook on a gentle heat until cooked through. Add a little chopped parsley and lemon juice to finish.

For The Paprika Potatoes

Heat a little oil in a non-stick pan. Season the potatoes with salt and paprika, then add to the pan. Cook gently on both sides until crisp and golden. Add a knob of butter to the pan and heat until foaming, then spoon it over the potatoes.

To Serve

Place the potatoes in the base of a warm plate or bowl. Spoon on the chorizo and set the hake on top. Place the prawns around and spoon on some of the butter. Drizzle with a little of the chorizo sauce to finish.

SALMON TERIYAKI, STIR FRIED ASIAN VEGETABLES

SERVES 4

 A bold Chardonnay; fruity but not too sweet to complement the teriyaki sauce!

Ingredients

4 x 180g salmon fillets

Teriyaki Sauce

1 tbsp oil
1 tbsp sesame oil
6 tbsp teriyaki sauce
2 tbsp rice wine vinegar
2 tbsp lime juice
2 tbsp honey

Stir Fried Asian Vegetables

vegetable oil (splash of)
½ red onion
½ red pepper
½ yellow pepper
½ green pepper
1 pak choi
20g beansprouts
1 tsp sesame oil
soy sauce (splash of)
½ lime (juice of)

To Serve

steamed jasmine rice
red chilli (sliced)
coriander
sesame seeds

Method

For The Teriyaki Sauce

Place all the ingredients into a saucepan and bring to the boil. Simmer for 10 minutes until reduced to a thick, glossy sauce.

For The Salmon

Preheat the oven to 175°C.

Heat a griddle pan or non-stick pan and when hot, place in the salmon steaks.

Cook on each side until the salmon is charred, then add to a clean pan with a little teriyaki sauce. Transfer to the oven for 4 minutes.

> **Chef's Tip**
>
> Add a splash of water to the salmon and teriyaki pan prior to cooking to prevent the sauce from burning.

For The Stir Fried Asian Vegetables

Slice the vegetables. Add a splash of vegetable oil to a wok, and when hot, add the vegetables. Cook for 1 minute, then add the sesame oil, soy sauce and lime juice.

To Serve

Spoon the teriyaki sauce on a warm serving plate and place the vegetables in a neat pile in the centre. Press the salmon fillets into a plate sprinkled with sesame seeds, then place the salmon on top of the vegetables. Serve with steamed jasmine rice, sliced red chilli and coriander.

086
DOXFORD HALL HOTEL & SPA

Chathill, Alnwick, Northumberland, NE67 5DN

01665 589 700
www.doxfordhall.com Twitter: @DoxfordHall
Facebook: Doxford Hall Hotel & Spa Instagram: doxford_hall

Having recently celebrated its 200th anniversary, Doxford Hall's elegance has certainly stood the test of time. Designed by John Dobson, the visionary much acclaimed for his work on Newcastle railway station, the classically-proportioned, mellow stone house, set in ten acres of grounds, was originally built for a wealthy, shipbuilding family.

Years on, when this Georgian manor house was being remodelled by a modern-day entrepreneur, to transform the once stately building into a luxury hotel, a craftsman joiner, George Runciman achieved wonders with his carpentry work. His contribution included a spectacular wooden staircase, handcrafted from local oak... and it's George who gives his name to the hotel's impressive 2 AA Rosette 'George Runciman Restaurant'.

Rather spectacular in design, with grand columns emphasising its high ceiling, ornate plasterwork, rows of generous sash windows, sumptuous drapes and glittering chandeliers; despite the grandeur, visitors note a warm and inviting ambience. This is certainly in part attributable to the lovely, friendly waiting staff.

Head chef, David Quinn, is a master of his culinary art, an established executive chef whose skills bring Northumberland's finest fayre into deliciously tasty modern British dishes, paired with a fine selection of wines.

Blessed with warm light, whether it be the morning sunlight through the sash windows, or soft glow candlelight reflecting upon the burgundy walls, the restaurant feels really welcoming. Never stuffy, it offers guests a relaxed, inviting space in which to enjoy fine dining and soak up the splendid Regency style.

Two centuries of hospitality, Northumberland's finest foods, friendly service and a stately dining room, which somehow manages to be both warm and inviting too, provides a winning formula!

LOCAL GOAT'S CURD, TEXTURES OF BEETROOT, SAVOURY GRANOLA

SERVES 4

🍷 *A light red wine: Granfort Cabernet Sauvignon, Pays d'Oc (France)*

Ingredients

400g local goat's curd

Textures Of Beetroot

6 beetroots
50ml balsamic vinegar
50g brown sugar
2 golden beetroots
oil (drizzle of)
salt (pinch of)

Savoury Granola

100g porridge oats
50g mixed seeds
20g pine nuts
oil (drizzle of)
20g honey
10g malt extract
10ml Henderson's Relish

Garnish

curly endive
pea shoots
rocket

Method

For The Textures Of Beetroot

Cover the beetroots in salted water and simmer until tender, about 1 hour. Remove the beetroots and gently peel off the skin. Thinly slice 2 of the beetroots, brush with balsamic vinegar and set aside. Blitz the remaining 4 beetroots in a food processor, adding the cooking *liquor* a little at a time, until you have a smooth, glossy purée. Reserve three-quarters of the purée and set aside. Add the remaining balsamic vinegar and brown sugar to the remaining quarter of purée and blitz again until smooth.

Preheat the oven to 160°C (fan).

Rub oil and salt over the golden beetroots and wrap in foil. Bake for 1 hour, allow to cool, then remove the skins.

For The Savoury Granola

Toast the oats and seeds in a heavy-based pan. Add a splash of oil to help colour them a little. Add the honey, malt and Henderson's Relish to the oat and seed mixture and stir continuously for 5 minutes, then spread onto a tray and allow to cool.

To Serve

Spread a swipe of the beetroot purée onto the plate, add dots of the beetroot and balsamic purée.

Using 2 large spoons, *quenelle* the goat's curd into torpedo shapes onto the plate. Sprinkle the granola around the dish in small piles. Cut the golden beetroot into batons or half moons and arrange at random around the plate, along with the beetroot discs (these can be curled to form cones if desired). Finish with sprigs of curly endive, pea shoots or rocket.

> **Chef's Tip**
>
> If the goat's curds are too wet, hang them in a muslin cloth or clean tea towel over a bowl for 4-5 hours; a lot of the water will come out.

PAN ROASTED JOHN DORY, OXTAIL CROQUETTE, PUMPKIN, SPLIT PUMPKIN SEED JUS

SERVES 4

 San Floriano Pinot Grigio, Friuli-Venezia Giulia (Italy)

Ingredients

Oxtail Croquette

2kg oxtail (separated at the joints)
2 carrots (roughly diced)
1 onion (roughly diced)
2 sticks celery (roughly diced)
500ml red wine
water (as required)
100g carrot, shallot and celeriac (finely diced)
50g plain flour
2 eggs (beaten with a splash of milk)
100g panko breadcrumbs
oil (for deep frying)

Pumpkin

1 medium pumpkin (peeled, halved)
water (splash of)
butter (knob of)
salt and pepper
30g pumpkin seeds (toasted)
30ml pumpkin seed oil
100g chanterelle mushrooms

John Dory

4 x 150g John Dory fillets
flour (to dust)
oil (splash of)
cold butter (knob of)
1 sprig thyme (optional)

To Serve

Tender-stem broccoli

Chef's Tip

John Dory can be quite hard to find but a lot of fish works well with a meat-based garnish; try using sea bass, halibut or cod as alternatives.

Method

For The Oxtail Croquette (Prepare in advance)
Preheat the oven to 150°C (fan).
Sear the oxtail pieces in a hot pan until deep brown, then transfer to a deep dish. In the same pan, sweat the roughly chopped vegetables, then add to the dish. Pour in the red wine and add enough water to fully submerge the meat. Cover and cook for 4 hours. Allow to cool slightly, then remove the meat from the *liquor*, reserving the liquid for later.

Pick all the meat from the bones, being careful to discard any gristle. Sweat the finely diced vegetables until softened. Add the meat and half the cooking *liquor* and reduce until sticky. Allow to cool.

Roll the mix into croquette shapes and freeze for 2 hours or until firm. Beat the eggs with a little milk, dust the croquettes in flour, then roll in the egg, then in the panko.

For The Pumpkin
Remove the seeds and strings from the pumpkin. Neatly dice one-third of the flesh and reserve. Roughly chop the remaining flesh.
Sweat the roughly chopped pumpkin in a heavy-based pan until it starts to soften. Add a little water and continue to cook slowly until the pumpkin is soft. Blitz in a blender whilst still warm, adding a knob of cold butter to form a glossy purée, season.
Reduce the remaining *liquor* by half to form a light sauce. Add half the pumpkin seeds and the pumpkin seed oil and reserve for later.

To Finish
Deep fry the croquettes (180°C) until golden brown, then place on a piece of kitchen towel to remove excess grease.
Lightly dust the John Dory fillets (skin-side) with flour and place, skin-side down, in a hot pan with a splash of oil. Fry until golden brown, removing the pan from the heat halfway through. Add a knob of cold butter and the thyme, if using, and gently turn each piece of fish over, allowing the residual heat of the pan to gently cook the flesh. This should take no more than 1-2 minutes.
Sweat off the neatly diced pumpkin until tender, add a knob of butter and the mushrooms and cook for a further 1 minute. Add the remaining pumpkin seeds and season.

To Serve
Spread the pumpkin purée onto the plate. Add the fish and pumpkin and mushroom mixture. Cut the ends off the croquette to reveal the meat and add to the plate. Finish with the split jus and serve with Tender-stem broccoli.

LEMON CREME BRULEE, TOASTED PINE NUT PASTRY, EARL GREY TEA MERINGUE

SERVES 4

 Sancerre, Domaine des Chaintres, Loire Valley (France)

Ingredients

Lemon Crème Brûlée

500ml double cream
150ml lemon juice
150g caster sugar
8 egg yolks

Toasted Pine Nut Pastry

1 sheet pre-rolled puff pastry
egg wash
40g pine nuts
30g golden granulated sugar

Earl Grey Tea Meringue

2 egg whites
60g caster sugar
15g loose leaf Earl Grey tea
2-3 tbsp boiling water

Garnish

candied lemon segments (optional)
10g pine nuts

To Serve

lemon meringue ice cream

5cm deep ovenproof dish (lined with a double layer of cling film)

Method

For The Lemon Crème Brûlée (Prepare ahead)

Preheat the oven to 110°C.

Warm the cream, lemon juice and sugar until the sugar is dissolved. Whisk the egg yolks in a large bowl, gradually adding the cream and lemon mixture. Pour the mixture into the prepared dish and bake for 40 minutes. Chill until completely set.

For The Toasted Pine Nut Pastry (Prepare ahead)

Preheat the oven to 180°C.

Brush the puff pastry with a little egg wash, sprinkle over the pine nuts and the golden granulated sugar. Place between 2 baking trays and bake for 15 minutes or until golden brown. Cut into strips.

For The Earl Grey Tea Meringue (Prepare ahead)

Preheat the oven to 110°C.

Beat the egg whites to stiff peaks. Continue whisking and slowly add the caster sugar, a little at a time. Add the boiling water to the tea leaves and allow to steep for 5 minutes. Strain, then pat dry with a piece of kitchen towel. Add the tea leaves to the meringue mixture and beat again until stiff peaks return. Pipe the mix onto a non-stick baking tray and bake in a cool oven for 1½ hours or until firm. Allow to cool.

To Serve

Using a round cookie cutter dipped in warm water, gently cut 4 rings of the crème brûlée, dust with a little sugar and lightly blow torch to form a golden crust. Garnish with the puff pastry strips, the meringues, a few pine nuts and some candied lemon segments. Serve with a *quenelle* of lemon meringue ice cream.

Chef's Tip

Some herbs or salad leaves work really well on desserts. Try adding small leaves of lemon balm or sorrel to finish the dish.

096
ESHOTT HALL

Eshott Hall, Morpeth, Northumberland, NE65 9EN

01670 895 884
www.eshotthall.co.uk Twitter: @eshotthall Facebook: Eshott Hall Instagram: eshott_hall

Eshott Hall is a timeless place, a Georgian gem of a property with its honey-coloured stone walls, and a welcoming entrance way, flanked by stone columns, which in the summer is draped with cascades of fragrant lilac wisteria.

As you drive through the iron gates and along the gravel driveway, bordered by mature trees and revealing striped lawns and abundant pots overflowing with colourful blooms, it's everything you might imagine a country home to be. Once the family home of Bainbridge, pioneer of England's first department store, Bainbridge's of Newcastle (now John Lewis), the Hall evokes memories of times gone by and a more gracious way of life.

Dining at Eshott is an elegant affair, amuse bouche, served in the elegant drawing room, accompanied by a gin cocktail, or perhaps a Pimms on the terrace? The evening dining room is intimate and hushed, allowing diners to savour the 2 AA Rosette à la carte dishes, crammed with local produce, rich pickings from Northumberland's renowned coasts, or fertile lands, topped with freshly-harvested salad leaves, vegetables, herbs and fruits from the walled kitchen garden just outside.

Morning time warrants its own dining room, flooded with natural sunlight for the occasion of a hearty breakfast, with rich tangy compôt of fragrant berries, fresh farm eggs and Craster kippers, among other goodies.

A stay at Eshott is a feast for the senses and you certainly won't be going home without feeling thoroughly nourished and restored. The charming and friendly staff makes your stay a real home-from-home experience, little wonder that many clients think fondly of Eshott as a special place to retreat time after time.

Savour the ambience of this elegant Georgian country house and its mouthwatering dishes, bursting with fresh flavour, when in-season produce is harvested from the Hall's own walled kitchen gardens.

WALLED GARDEN
&
TENNIS COURT

PIGEON, SCOTCH EGG, BEETROOT

SERVES 4

Rioja - Pigeon has a strong taste, so you need a wine that doesn't get lost but also something that isn't overpowering. Rioja is a good match as it's a full-flavoured red but with fruity aromas and doesn't hold a tannin taste.

Ingredients

Scotch Egg

4 quail eggs
450g sausagemeat
4 rings black pudding
2 large eggs (beaten)
100ml whole milk
plain flour (to *pane*)
panko breadcrumbs (to *pane*)
oil (to deep fry)

Pigeon

4 pigeon breasts
salt and pepper

Beetroot Glaze

200ml beetroot juice (reduced by three-quarters)

To Serve

pickled beetroot
confit beetroot
beetroot chutney

Method

For The Scotch Egg

Bring a pan of water to the boil. Add the quail eggs and cook for 2½ minutes. Transfer immediately into iced water. Peel when cold.

Combine the sausagemeat with the black pudding, mix well, then roll into 4 balls. Press a thumb into each ball, insert a quail egg and gently mould the sausage mix over the top. Combine the eggs and milk in a bowl. *Pane* the balls by rolling first in the flour, then the egg mix, finishing with the panko breadcrumbs. Deep fry the Scotch egg (160°C) for 5 minutes.

> **Chef's Tip**
>
> Add a splash of vinegar to the boiling water pan for the quails' eggs, it makes them easier to peel.

For The Pigeon

Heat a frying pan. Season with pigeon breasts, then place in the hot pan and sear on each side for 1 minute. Leave to rest for 1 minute.

To Serve

Paint the plate with the beetroot glaze. Slice the Scotch eggs in half, the yolks should be runny. Cut the pigeon breasts in half and place on the plate. Serve with additional beetroot elements as desired.

TURBOT

SERVES 4

🍷 *Chardonnay or Chablis - Turbot is meaty in texture and flavour but has a mild taste; you can't go wrong with a crisp Chardonnay or the fresh, delicate taste of a good Chablis!*

Ingredients

100g puy lentils

Vegetables And Sauce

8 king oyster mushrooms
200g pancetta (diced)
500ml chicken stock
4 potatoes (diced)
80g butter (diced)
16 baby leeks

Turbot

4 x 100g turbot fillets
butter (knob of)

Garnish

celeriac crisps

Method

For The Puy Lentils

Cook the lentils in boiling water until soft, about 10 minutes. Leave to cool and set aside.

For The Vegetables And Sauce

Chargrill the oyster mushrooms for 30 seconds, then add to a pan with the pancetta, chicken stock and diced potato. Cook for 8 minutes until the potato is soft, then add the diced butter to slightly thicken the sauce.

For The Turbot

Pan fry the turbot in butter over a medium heat in a non-stick pan for 30 seconds on each side. Remove the fillets from the pan and place on a baking tray.

Chef's Tip

Season the fish immediately before you pan fry it. If you season it before, it will draw the moisture out of the fish.

To Serve

Preheat the oven to 180°C.

Add the lentils to the sauce along with the baby leeks and reheat gently. Place the turbot in the oven for 3-4 minutes. Serve as pictured, garnished with celeriac crisps.

FIG STRUDEL

SERVES 6

🍷 *Moscatel dessert wine - This wine is known to pair especially well with pastry dishes. It's one of the bolder tasting dessert wines on the market today. It handles the hints of red wine, ginger and cinnamon perfectly.*

Ingredients

1 vanilla pod (scraped)
3 cloves
3 star anise
1 tbsp ground ginger
1 tbsp ground cinnamon
1 orange (zest and juice of)
200g sugar
200ml water
200ml red wine
250g butter
10 plums
1 pack filo sheets
10 figs (thinly sliced)

Method

To Make The Fig Strudel (Prepare ahead)

Place the vanilla, cloves, star anise, ginger, cinnamon, orange, sugar, water and wine in a pan and bring to a simmer. Add the plums to the stock syrup and gently poach the plums until they have softened and turned a purple colour. Leave to cool, then slice the plums thinly.

Melt the butter, then brush a sheet of filo pastry with the butter. Place another sheet on top, brush with butter and repeat one more time.

Place lines of fig slices side by side across the filo up to half way. Lay the sliced plums on top of the figs. Roll the pastry from the side which has the filling on, then brush with butter. Wrap in cling film, then freeze. The strudel may be cut from frozen to your desired size.

Preheat the oven to 200°C.

Bake the strudel, from frozen, for 15-20 minutes.

To Serve

Serve as pictured.

> **Chef's Tip**
>
> When melting the butter for the strudel, only use the *clarified butter* on the top or the milk will be too salty.

106
HEADLAM HALL

Headlam, Near Gainford, Darlington, DL2 3HA

01325 730 238
www.headlamhall.co.uk

This authentic country house hotel, spa and golf course stands amidst its own picturesque and rolling farmland on the Durham and North Yorkshire border, close to the River Tees. Owned by the Robinson family, who have been farming in Headlam for four generations, it is perhaps no surprise that the food offering is strongly based on the use of ingredients that are either local or with excellent provenance. The Hall gardens provide herbs, fruits and vegetables to the kitchen team in season and long-established local suppliers work closely with the chefs to bring the best of the region's produce to the plate.

The interiors combine fabulous period features with contemporary country-living design. Guests can relax in the eclectic Library Bar or take a seat by the huge open fire in the impressive main lounge. The restaurant is a stylish and airy orangery that protrudes into a walled terrace and private dining options are available in the adjacent Olive Room and Panelled Room. Larger dinner parties can be catered for in either the Drawing Room which overlooks the main lawns or across the courtyard in the Coach House, a self-contained venue with its own bar and lounge area.

Head chef Derek Thomson, along with the skilled kitchen team, create dishes that reflect the rural location and heritage of Headlam Hall and the strong relationships with local suppliers.

SALTED COD, BUTTERNUT VELOUTE, PICKLED BUTTERNUT

SERVES 4

 Grüner Veltliner (Austria)

Ingredients

Butternut Velouté

100g butter
2 onions (roughly chopped)
2 cloves garlic (chopped)
1kg butternut squash (chopped)
2 litres vegetable stock
200ml double cream

Pickled Butternut Squash

50ml water
20g sugar
100ml distilled vinegar
200g butternut shavings

Salted Cod

20g juniper berries
30g Maldon sea salt
4 x 90g cod loin portions (skinned)
400ml olive oil

Garnish

pumpkin seeds (toasted)
olive oil (drizzle of)

Method

For The Butternut Velouté

Melt the butter, add the onions and garlic and fry until soft. Add the squash and continue to cook for 5 minutes, stirring occasionally. Pour in the stock and simmer until the squash is fully cooked. Add the cream and slowly reduce for about 20 minutes. Blitz until smooth, then pass through a fine sieve. Season to taste.

> **Chef's Tip**
>
> Be careful not to season the velouté too much as it could become too salty when served with the salted cod.

For The Pickled Butternut Squash

Gently heat the water, sugar and vinegar in a pan until the sugar has dissolved. Pour the mix over the butternut and leave to cool.

For The Salted Cod

Preheat the oven to 180°C (fan).

Roast the juniper berries for 5 minutes, then blitz with the salt. Use the mix to season the cod, then wrap tightly in cling film and leave for 30 minutes in the fridge.

Heat the oil to 52-56°C. Rinse the salt mix off the cod, then pat it dry. Place into the oil for 15-20 minutes. Leave to rest for 5 minutes.

To Serve

Place the velouté into a bowl. Add the cod to the centre, then place the pickled butternut around the fish. Finish with a drizzle of the olive oil and some toasted pumpkin seeds.

PAN FRIED BREAST OF DUCK, FIG PUREE, RED CABBAGE, ROAST BABY CARROTS, POTATO LACES, CITRUS & TARRAGON JUS

SERVES 4

Pinot Noir
(New Zealand)

Ingredients

Citrus And Tarragon Jus

2 duck carcases
2 bottles red wine (Malbec)
1 orange (zest of)
2 sprigs tarragon (chopped)

Fig Purée

200g sugar
300g ripe figs

Red Cabbage

500g red cabbage (finely sliced)
300ml red wine
3 cloves
1 star anise
200g sugar
30ml vinegar

Potato Laces

2 Rooster potatoes (peeled)
vegetable oil (for deep frying)
sea salt

Roast Baby Carrots

200g baby carrots (cleaned, trimmed)
oil (drizzle of)
salt and pepper
1 sprig thyme (picked)

Duck

4 duck breasts
oil (drizzle of)
salt and pepper

Chef's Tip

Add sultanas and redcurrant jelly to the cabbage for a sweeter flavour.

Method

For The Citrus And Tarragon Jus (Prepare ahead)
Preheat the oven to 185°C (fan).
Roast the duck bones for 35 minutes, turning occasionally to get even colour. Once golden, add to a large stock pan, cover with cold water, bring to the boil and add 1 bottle of wine.
Skim any impurities from the top and simmer gently for 7 hours, skimming every 30 minutes or so. Pass the stock through fine muslin cloth. Refrigerate overnight or for 8 hours. You can make the stock in advance and keep in the fridge or freezer.
Reduce the remaining bottle of wine in a heavy-based pan until a thick syrupy consistency. Skim off any fat that has set on the stock. Add the stock to the wine syrup and bring to a rapid boil. Reduce by about half, skimming off any remaining fat. Add the orange zest and chopped tarragon.

For The Fig Purée
Make a dry caramel with the sugar. Add the figs and cook until all the liquid has evaporated. Blitz, then pass through a fine sieve. Store in a squeezy bottle.

For The Red Cabbage
Place all the ingredients in a pan and cook on a low heat until the liquid has reduced, stirring occasionally.

For The Potato Laces
Put the potatoes through a spiralizer, lightly oil and season with salt. Pick out strands and place in the fryer one by one, gathering all the strands to make loose nests. Fry until golden brown for about 4-5 minutes, then drain on absorbent paper and season with a little more salt.

For The Roast Baby Carrots
Preheat the oven to 180°C (fan).
Toss the carrots in the oil and season with salt and pepper. Place on a baking tray and sprinkle with thyme. Roast in the oven for 15-20 minutes.

For The Duck
Heat a frying pan with a little oil. Lightly score the skin of the duck, season and place, skin-side down, in the pan on a medium heat for about 4-5 minutes. Turn the duck over and cook for a further 5 minutes, depending on how pink you like it. Remove from the pan and leave to rest whilst plating.

To Serve
Serve as pictured.

CHOCOLATE & MARMALADE FONDANT

SERVES 6

Elysium Black Muscat (USA)

Ingredients

Salted Caramel

300g caster sugar
10g Maldon sea salt
100g butter
200ml double cream

Honeycomb

315g caster sugar
125g liquid glucose
50g honey
60ml water
15g bicarbonate of soda

Vanilla Cream

200ml double cream
2 tbsp icing sugar
1 vanilla pod (seeds of)

Chocolate And Marmalade Fondant

50g white chocolate
50g dark chocolate (54%)
70g thick cut marmalade
125g caster sugar
125g butter
4 free-range medium eggs
155g plain flour (sifted)

20cm square tin (greased with butter)
6 dariole moulds (greased with butter and sugar)

Method

For The Salted Caramel

Place the sugar in a heavy-based pan and stir over a medium heat until golden brown. Add the salt and stir thoroughly. Mix in the butter and stir until incorporated. Pour in the cream and bring back to the boil. Pass through a fine *chinois* and decant into a squeezy bottle.

For The Honeycomb

Mix the sugar, liquid glucose, honey and water in a pan and stir over a gentle heat until dissolved.

Once completely melted, turn up the heat a little and simmer until you have an amber-coloured caramel or until it reaches 147°C on a sugar thermometer. Turn off the heat, add the bicarbonate and beat it until it has all disappeared and the mix is foaming. Add to the greased tray immediately, being careful as it will be very hot. Leave to set for 1 hour, then break into pieces.

For The Vanilla Cream

Whisk the ingredients together until soft peaks.

For The Chocolate And Marmalade Fondant

Preheat the oven to 190°C (fan).

Melt the chocolates, marmalade, sugar and butter together over a *bain-marie*. Remove from the heat, add the eggs and mix thoroughly with a whisk. Gently fold in the flour. Divide the mixture between the dariole moulds and bake for 9 minutes. Serve immediately.

> **Chef's Tip**
> If making the fondants in advance, refrigerate before cooking and add 2 minutes to the cooking time.

To Assemble

Crumble some honeycomb onto a plate. Turn out the fondant and place on the plate along with some bigger pieces of honeycomb. Squeeze 3 large dots of salted caramel around the plate and finish with a spoon of vanilla cream.

116
THE JOLLY FISHERMAN

Haven Hill, Craster, Northumberland, NE66 3TR

01665 576 461
www.thejollyfishermancraster.co.uk Twitter: @TheJollyCraster

The Jolly Fisherman is an award-winning pub based in Craster, a small fishing village on the Northumbrian coast. It feels like so much more than a pub; it combines stunning sea views with a delicious, relaxed, gastro food menu It is charming and full of character, with low beams, stone flagged floors and a roaring fire to keep you warm in the winter months. The restaurant has a view to rival any in the country and in the summer months, you can enjoy the terrace or the beer garden with its spectacular views overlooking Craster Harbour.

The 'Jolly' was established in 1847 by Charles Archbold and has grown in size and reputation ever since with locals, walkers and day-trippers.

The ethos is to buy local, with fresh crab and lobsters being landed a mere stone's throw by the boats in the harbour and the ethically produced meats coming from the surrounding area and North Yorkshire. With classically French trained, executive head chef Kevin Mulraney heading up the kitchen team, the quality of food being served is reaching greater heights and adding to the growing reputation.

Special attention is paid to the drinks too. You can be assured of a great pint of real ale at The Jolly Fisherman. The regular cask beers, Workie Ticket and Black Sheep, stand alongside specially selected monthly guest ales and an interesting and varied wine menu complements the food beautifully.

The Jolly Fisherman, a tastefully refurbished pub with tradition and character at its heart.

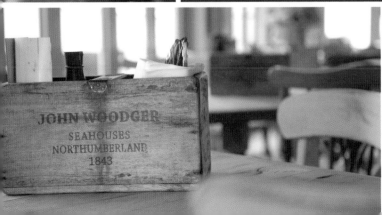

JOHN WOODGER
SEAHOUSES
NORTHUMBERLAND
1843

KIPPER SCOTCH EGG, TRUFFLE MAYONNAISE

SERVES 4

 Pol Roger, Brut NV Champagne
(France)

Ingredients

Kipper Pâté

4 kipper fillets
½ lemon
120ml water
125g full-fat cream cheese
50g creamed horseradish
25ml double cream
2 pinches cracked black pepper

Kipper Scotch Egg

4 large free-range eggs
500g kipper pâté
200g mashed potato
100g plain flour
250ml egg wash
200g panko breadcrumbs
oil (for deep frying)

Truffle Mayonnaise

30g white truffle
125ml mayonnaise

To Serve

frisée lettuce
pea shoots
4 cheese straws

Method

For The Kipper Pâté

Preheat the oven to 160°C (fan).

Place the kipper fillets, lemon and water in an ovenproof dish, cover with tin foil and steam roast for 20 minutes. Remove from the oven and leave to cool.

Remove the skin from the fish and place the flesh in a mixing bowl. Break up the flesh, then fold in the cream cheese and horseradish. Season with cracked black pepper. Fold through the double cream and refrigerate.

For The Kipper Scotch Egg

Cook the eggs in salted, boiling water; 6 minutes for runny, 7 minutes for set. Remove from the water, then refresh in iced water. Peel the eggs.

Combine the pâté with the mashed potato. Divide the kipper mix into 4 and cover evenly around the eggs, doing one at a time. *Pane* each egg by rolling in flour, dipping in egg wash, then rolling in the breadcrumbs. Deep fry at 172°C for 6 minutes. Remove from the oil and keep warm.

For The Truffle Mayonnaise

Finely grate the truffle into the mayonnaise and stir to combine.

> **Chef's Tip**
>
> If you can't source real truffle, substitute with white truffle oil and finely grate a chestnut mushroom into the mayonnaise.

To Assemble

Place the mayonnaise on a board or plate, then swipe with the back of a spoon. Cut the eggs in half. Garnish each plate with frisée lettuce, pea shoots and a cheese straw.

'POSH PEA & HAM SOUP'
HAM HOCK, PISTACHIO & MUSTARD
TERRINE, PEA VELOUTE, PEASE PUDDING

SERVES 4

Chablis, Frèvre Burgundy
(France)

Ingredients

Ham Hock And Stock

1 ham hock
water (to cover)
1 stick celery (roughly chopped)
1 carrot (chopped)
2 bay leaves
1 lemon (zest of)

Terrine

ham hock meat (shredded)
1 tbsp mustard seeds
1 tbsp chopped parsley
2 tbsp pistachios (crushed)
salt and pepper (to taste)

Pea Velouté

reserved ham hock stock (less 250ml for pease pudding)
200g split peas
200g frozen peas

Pease Pudding

250ml reserved ham hock stock
100g split yellow peas
½ tsp butter (soft)

Garnish

1 tbsp pistachios (crushed)
pea shoots

Method

For The Ham Hock (Prepare ahead)

Cover the ham hock with water, add the other ingredients, bring to the boil and simmer for 3 hours until the meat is falling away from the bone. Remove the meat and allow to cool. Once the meat is cool enough to handle, pull the meat into strands. Drain the stock and set aside for the velouté and pease pudding.

For The Terrine (Prepare ahead)

Combine all the ingredients in a mixing bowl. Mix well, then turn onto cling film. Roll into a log, about 16cm long, and tie both ends. Refrigerate for 3 hours to set.

> **Chef's Tip**
>
> When you roll the terrine, prick the cling film with a cocktail stick to allow air to escape in order to get a tight log.

For The Pea Velouté

Measure out 250ml of the reserved ham stock and set aside for the pease pudding.

Add the split peas to the stock and cook for 1½ hours over a low heat. Top up with water if the soup looks too thick. Add the frozen peas and simmer for 1 minute. Blend until smooth. Check the consistency and seasoning. Keep warm.

For The Pease Pudding

Gently heat the stock with the split peas and bring to the boil. Simmer for 45 minutes, then blend until smooth. Stir in the butter, remove from the heat and keep warm.

To Assemble The Dish

Cut a slice of terrine 4cm long and place in the centre of a soup plate. Pour the velouté around the terrine, then *quenelle* the pease pudding on top of the terrine. Sprinkle with crushed pistachios and finish with some pea shoots.

ASIAN SPICED HAKE, CURRY MAYONNAISE, SPINACH, CAULIFLOWER FRITTER, BHAJI, BOMBAY POTATO

SERVES 4

 Sancerre, Pierre Martin, Loire (France)

Ingredients

4 x 170g hake fillets

Asian Spice

1 tsp mild Madras curry powder
1 tsp garam masala, 1 tsp coriander seeds
1 tsp pink peppercorns,
2 cloves garlic (peeled)
½ tsp desiccated coconut
1 tsp rock sea salt, ¼ tsp red chilli flakes

Bhaji

1 medium-sized white onion (halved, thinly sliced)
125g self-raising flour (sifted)
ground turmeric (pinch of)
mild Madras curry powder (pinch of)
200ml whole milk, oil (for deep frying)

Cauliflower Fritter

570ml cold water, 12 ice cubes,
1 large egg , ½ tsp turmeric
125g self-raising flour (sifted, plus extra for dusting)
4 raw cauliflower florets (about 2cm square)

Bombay Potato

2 medium-sized Maris Pipers (peeled cut into
2cm chunks), ½ tsp salt
½ tsp ground turmeric, 2 tsp garam masala
1 tsp black mustard seeds
4 cherry tomatoes (quartered)
1 small onion (finely diced), 3 tbsp rapeseed oil

Curry Mayonnaise

4 tbsp mayonnaise
1 tsp mild Madras curry powder
¼ lemon (juice of), ½ tsp ground turmeric

Spinach

200g baby spinach leaves, salt and pepper
freshly grated nutmeg

Method

For The Asian Spice
Crush all the ingredients to a fine powder with a pestle and mortar.

For The Bhaji
Place the onion in a mixing bowl. Add the other ingredients, except the milk and oil, and evenly coat the onions. Add the milk, mixing with a fork, then set aside to rest for 20 minutes. Roll the mix into 4 balls. Deep fry for 6 minutes at 175°C. Remove and keep warm.

For The Cauliflower Fritter
Add the ice to the water and set aside for 20 minutes to become ice cold.
Lightly whip the egg with a fork in a mixing bowl until it is nearly combined.
Stir the turmeric into the flour, then add to the egg. Measure 225ml of the iced water and stir into the mix, being careful not to overwhip; it should still look a little lumpy.
Dust the florets with flour, then coat in batter. Deep fry for 6 minutes at 175°C until golden brown. Remove and keep warm.

For The Bombay Potato
Preheat the oven to 200°C (fan).
Place the potatoes in a saucepan and cover with water. Add the salt and turmeric, bring to the boil and simmer for 5 minutes. Drain the potatoes, then toss them in the other ingredients, ensuring all the potatoes are well coated. Turn out into a roasting tin and bake for 20 minutes until crispy. Remove and keep warm.

For The Hake
Preheat the oven to 200°C (fan).
Dust the fillets with the Asian spice and allow to marinate for at least 20 minutes. The powder will rehydrate and resemble paste.
Place the fillets on a parchment lined tray and bake, uncovered, for 8 minutes. Remove and keep warm.

For The Curry Mayonnaise
Cream all the ingredients together until smooth.

For The Spinach
Blanch the spinach in salted, boiling water for 5 seconds, remove and drain. Season with salt, pepper and ground nutmeg. Divide into 4 and keep warm.

To Assemble The Dish
Drag some of the curry mayonnaise along the plates with the back of a spoon. Place a spinach portion in the centre of each plate and top with the hake. Arrange the Bombay potato, bhaji and cauliflower fritter around the fish.

BEEF FILLET, WILD MUSHROOM RISOTTO & GRATIN, CONFIT GARLIC, ONION PUREE

SERVES 4

🍷 Madiran, L'Origine Château Laplace
(France)

Ingredients

Wild Mushroom Gratin

1 shallot (finely diced), 1 clove garlic (crushed)
olive oil (drizzle of)
100g mixed wild mushrooms (chopped)
100g chestnut mushrooms (chopped)
2 tbsp white wine
4 tbsp double cream
sea salt and cracked black pepper
1 large egg yolk
1 tbsp chopped chives

Confit Garlic

12 cloves garlic (peeled), 125ml rapeseed oil

Wild Mushroom Risotto

120g risotto rice
2 tbsp garlic oil
50g wild mushrooms (chopped)
50g chestnut mushrooms (chopped)
150ml chicken stock
40g Berwick Edge cheese (grated)
½ tsp horseradish
1 tbsp chopped parsley
30ml double cream

Onion Purée

2 medium white onions (sliced)
100ml double cream
¼ tsp English mustard powder
60g butter (diced)

Beef Fillet

4 fillet steaks, 180g each 4cm high
olive oil (drizzle of)
salt and pepper
2 tbsp grated Parmesan

Garnish

1 bunch watercress, beef shin bones
seasonal vegetables

Method

For The Wild Mushroom Gratin

Sauté the shallot and garlic in olive oil then add the mushrooms and cook until softened. Add the white wine and cook until dry, then add the cream and season. Bring to the boil, then remove from the heat and allow to cool. Stir in the egg yolk and chives.

For The Confit Garlic

Place the garlic cloves in a pan and add the oil. Heat for 10 minutes until the garlic is golden brown. Remove and keep warm.

For The Wild Mushroom Risotto

Cook the rice for 8 minutes in boiling, salted water, then refresh. Fry the mushrooms in the garlic oil until soft, then add all the other ingredients, except the cream. Heat through, stirring constantly. Add the cream, remove from the heat and keep warm.

For The Onion Purée

Place the onions in a pan with the cream and simmer until softened, about 5 minutes. Add the mustard, then blend until smooth. Stir in the butter, remove from the heat and keep warm.

For The Beef Fillet

Pan fry the fillets in a little olive oil. Cook for 2-3 minutes, turning constantly to seal the meat. Remove from the pan, season and allow to cool.

> **Chef's Tip**
> Use a long piece of fillet 600g; roll in cling film, tie the ends and refrigerate. This helps to keep a round steak.

To Finish And To Serve

Preheat the oven to 220°C (fan).

Place the steaks on a tray, top with the gratin and cover with grated Parmesan. Place in centre of the oven and bake for 8 minutes (rare), 10 minutes (medium rare) or 12 minutes (medium). Remove and let the steaks rest for 8 minutes, keep warm.

Swipe a tablespoon of onion purée on each plate and set the steak on top. Fill a beef shin bone with the risotto and place on the purée. Add the *confit* garlic cloves, watercress and vegetables of your choice.

STICKY TOFFEE PUDDING, BUTTERSCOTCH SAUCE, VANILLA POD ICE CREAM, LITTLE TOFFEE APPLES

SERVES 4

 Port, dry sherry, Madeira or whisky liqueur

Ingredients

Sticky Toffee Pudding

175g pitted dates
2 tsp bicarbonate of soda
375ml boiling water
85g unsalted butter (softened)
114g soft dark brown sugar
2 tsp baking powder
227g plain flour (sifted)
2 large eggs
2 tsp vanilla essence

Vanilla Pod Ice Cream

8 large eggs (separated)
227g icing sugar
225g caster sugar
2 vanilla pods (seeds of)
1 litre double cream

Little Toffee Apples

400g caster sugar
100ml water
1 tsp white wine vinegar
4 tbsp golden syrup
8 dwarf red Bramley apples (available from good delicatessens)

Butterscotch Sauce

250g butter
225g soft dark brown sugar
500ml double cream

8 bamboo cocktail sticks
30cm x 11cm x 8cm loaf tin (lined)

Method

For The Sticky Toffee Pudding

Place the dates in a tub, add the bicarbonate of soda, cover with the boiling water and leave to soak for 30 minutes.
Beat the butter and sugar until creamy and fluffy. Sift the baking powder with the flour.
Add 1 egg to the butter and beat on a medium speed. Add half the flour and half the dates and combine well. Add the remaining egg, flour, dates including the *liquor* and vanilla essence.
Preheat the oven to 180°C (fan).
Spoon a layer of toffee sauce into the bottom of the loaf tin. Top with the cake mixture. Bake for 20 minutes, then lower the heat to 150°C (fan) and bake for a further 30 minutes. Remove from the oven and turn upside down onto a cooling rack. Keep warm.

For The Vanilla Pod Ice Cream (Prepare ahead)

You will need 3 mixing bowls and an electric whisk.
In one bowl, whip the egg whites to form stiff peaks, then fold in the icing sugar.
In the second bowl, beat the egg yolks, caster sugar and vanilla seeds until fluffy and smooth.
In the third bowl, whip the double cream to stiff peaks.
With a metal spoon, fold the egg yolk mix through the cream, then fold the beaten egg whites into the cream and yolk mixture. Do this with large swooping folds to keep the air in.
Pour into a plastic airtight container and freeze for at least 6 hours. No need to churn or stir.

For The Little Toffee Apples

Place the sugar and water in a saucepan and heat gently until the sugar has dissolved. Add the vinegar and syrup. Heat to 150°C ('hard crack') and hold at this temperature. Spike each apple with a cocktail stick and dip into the caramel. Place on parchment paper to set.

For The Butterscotch Sauce

Place all the ingredients in a pan, gently heat, then bring to the boil. Simmer for 8-10 minutes until thick and creamy. Remove from the heat and keep warm.

To Assemble The Dish

Cut the pudding into 4 portions and place in the centre of each plate. Make a little crater in the top with the back of a spoon, pour some sauce over the pudding and place 2 toffee apples around it. Finally, roll a ball of ice cream and sit it in the crater on top of the pudding.

GLAZED LEMON TART, CHOCOLATE GANACHE, CLOTTED CREAM & AMARETTO MILKSHAKE

SERVES 8

 Amaretto or Limoncello

Ingredients

Pastry

175g plain flour
40g icing sugar
salt (pinch of)
75g butter (soft)
1 large egg yolk (reserve the white for later)
1 tbsp water

Lemon Filling

5 lemons (juice and zest of)
5 large eggs (lightly beaten)
150g caster sugar (plus extra to finish)
175ml double cream

Ganache

110g dark chocolate (70%)
110ml double cream
1 tbsp almond essence

Clotted Cream And Amaretto Milkshake

100g clotted cream
200ml whole milk
2 tbsp double cream
1 shot Amaretto

To Serve

2 tbsp caster sugar
clotted cream
raspberries
icing sugar

20cm sponge tin (lined with parchment paper)
42cm square piece tin foil

Method

For The Pastry

Combine the flour, icing sugar and salt with the butter, rub until it resembles breadcrumbs. Add the yolk and water to form a dough. Wrap in cling film and allow to rest for 20 minutes in the fridge. Roll out the pastry to a 30cm circle and transfer to the tin. Press in firmly and cut the rim to shape. Prick the base of the pastry with a fork and place in the freezer for 30 minutes.

> **Chef's Tip**
>
> Use type 45 (pastry flour) or substitute with type 55 (bread flour) for a less fragile pastry.

For The Lemon Filling

Zest the lemons and squeeze enough juice to give 225ml. Crack the eggs into a jug, add the sugar and lightly whip together. Add the lemon juice and zest followed by the cream and whisk lightly.

To Cook The Tart

Preheat the oven to 190°C (fan).

Place the frozen pastry case on a baking sheet. Cover the base with the tin foil, fold the edges in and crumple it against the sides to support them. Bake for 15 minutes, remove from the oven and carefully remove the foil. Brush the egg white all over the pastry. Return to the oven for 7 minutes, then remove and lower the temperature to 180°C (fan). Pour the filling into the case and bake for 30 minutes. The tart should be set and springy in the middle. Allow to cool.

For The Ganache

Place all the ingredients in a bowl and melt over a *bain-marie*. Allow to cool.

For The Clotted Cream And Amaretto Milkshake

Place all the ingredients in a measuring jug and whip until a rich creamy foam is created. Serve immediately.

To Serve

Sprinkle the tart with caster sugar and blow torch the sugar until a brûlée glaze is achieved. Place in the centre of your plate, spoon a *quenelle* of clotted cream and ganache onto the plate and serve with the milkshake. Garnish with a few raspberries dusted with icing sugar.

132
LOLLO ROSSO

40 Bridge Street, Morpeth, NE61 1NL

01670 514 111
www.lollorossoitalia.com Twitter: @lollorossoitalia

Nestled in the picturesque Northumbrian town of Morpeth, Lollo Rosso is a dynamic and popular restaurant specialising in contemporary Italian cuisine. Best known for its exuberant atmosphere and high quality menu, it is a much loved favourite amongst locals.

Established in 2015, Lollo Rosso's growth is testament to the vision of its long-time friends and partners. Built on a fundamental love of food, it offers diners a unique blend of wholesome Italian cooking and vibrant hospitality. Earning themselves a steadfast following, the team recognised the need to expand their offer to meet the ever growing demand and, after only two years, moved to one of Morpeth's principle buildings: the beautifully refurbished 'Smailes' ironmongers, which boasts a contemporary, industrial interior, paying tribute to the site's significant heritage within the community.

Exuding the warmth and vivacity of its owners, Lollo Rosso is alive with energy from the moment it opens its doors. Drop in for a midweek lunch or dinner and you'll enjoy the buzz of a metropolitan eatery, or book for a weekend evening and feel the electric atmosphere with live singers and dancing long into the night.

Head chef Enzo Saurino has been cooking with the same love for food for forty years. You can sense the influence of Ischia in the menu, you can feel the drive of his kitchen team from the open pass, and this transfers to the restaurant and helps create the atmosphere for the diner.

Guaranteed to be greeted with open arms, its trio of owners bring a unique twist to the traditional Italian concept. Hailing from the beautiful islands of Ischia, Cuba and Andros, Giovanni, Miguel and Nikos bring their vast experience, passion and cultural hospitality to the warmth of Lollo Rosso.

With delicious, freshly prepared, authentic Italian food and a vibrant atmosphere - Lollo Rosso is the place everybody is talking about.

INSALATA CALDA DI MARE

SERVES 4

 Santa Cristina Capsula Viola, Tuscany (Italy)

Ingredients

Insalata Calda Di Mare

2 shallots (diced)
olive oil (drizzle of)
1 sprig thyme
3 large potatoes (peeled, finely chopped)
2 tbsp white wine
fish stock (as required)
salt and pepper (to season)
1 sack squid ink
1 bud saffron
40g garden peas (blended)
1 tbsp tomato purée
fresh mussels (large handful of)
fresh clams (large handful of)
8 king sized scallops
1 fresh squid
8 king prawns

Garnish

fresh chervil

Method

For The Insalata Calda Di Mare

Sauté the shallots in a drizzle of olive oil in a large pan until softened. Stir in the potatoes and thyme and continue to cook until the potatoes are tender. Add the white wine and cook until reduced. Pour in enough fish stock to cover the potatoes and shallots. Transfer to a powerful blender, season and blend until smooth. Divide the mixture between 4 separate pans.

In the first pan, add the squid ink. In the second, add the saffron. Add the blended peas to the third pan and finally the tomato purée to the fourth pan.

Steam the mussels and clams until the shells open, discarding any that don't open. When cool enough to handle, remove from the shells and set aside.

Pan fry the scallops, squid and king prawns in a large pan in a drizzle of olive oil.

Chef's Tip

Only use the very freshest of seafood for this dish
Discard any mussels or clams that don't shut tight when tapped prior to cooking.

To Serve

Heat 4 plates for serving. Decorate the plates by drizzling the 4 sauces onto the plates. Finish by adding the seafood and garnish with fresh chervil. Serve immediately.

LOBSTER THERMIDOR

SERVES 2

🍷 *Principi di Butera Insolia, Sicily*
(Italy)

Method

For The Lobster

Preheat the oven to 180°C.

Bake the lobster in the oven for 5 minutes, then remove and set aside.

For The Thermidor Sauce

Sauté the spring onions and mushrooms in a drizzle of oil over a medium heat for 3 minutes. Add the brandy, then *flambé* to burn off the alcohol. Pour in the cream and fish stock, add the tarragon and reduce for 3 minutes. Mix in the Dijon mustard and season with salt, pepper and nutmeg to taste.

> **Chef's Tip**
> Only use fresh tarragon for this dish. The freshness of the herb makes a huge impact to the flavour of the sauce.

To Serve

Top both halves of the lobster with the sauce, then sprinkle with Parmesan. Place the lobster under a medium heat grill and cook for 5 minutes. Garnish and serve as pictured.

Ingredients

1 whole lobster (split into 2 halves)

Thermidor Sauce
2 spring onions (sliced)
75g wild mushrooms (diced)
20ml cooking oil
30ml brandy
75ml double cream
50ml fish stock
10g fresh tarragon (chopped)
½ tbsp Dijon mustard
nutmeg (pinch of)
salt and pepper

To Serve
30g Parmesan (grated)
edible flowers
fresh parsley

TIRAMISU

SERVES 4

🍷 *Türk Muskateller Beerenauslese, Stratzing (Austria)*

Ingredients

Tiramisu

2 large eggs
100g sugar
100g mascarpone cheese
50ml marsala wine
200ml coffee
8 savoiardi biscuit fingers
cocoa powder (to dust)

To Serve

chocolate sauce
whipped cream
sugar work
edible flowers

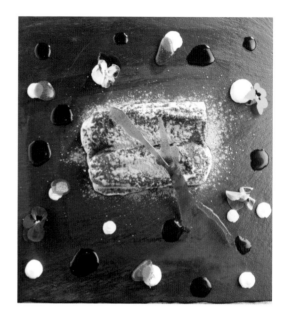

Method

For The Tiramisu

Separate the egg yolks and whites into 2 separate bowls, then add half the sugar to the yolks and the other half to the whites. Whisk for 1 minute each.

Combine the mascarpone and marsala, stir into the yolk and sugar mixture, then carefully fold in the whisked egg white mixture. It should resemble Chantilly cream.

Dip the savoiardi fingers individually in the coffee and place half of them in a layer in the bottom of a dish. Place the cream mixture on top of the biscuits. Repeat this process.

To Serve

Serve the tiramisu as pictured, dusted with cocoa powder and decorated as desired.

Chef's Tip

A classic Italian dessert which is ideal for any dinner party as it can be made a few hours in advance

142
THE ORANGERY AT ROCKLIFFE HALL

Rockliffe Hall, Hurworth on Tees, Darlington, County Durham, DL2 2DU

01325 729 999
www.rockliffehall.com Twitter: @RockliffeHall @orangery_rh Facebook: facebook.com/rockliffehall

The Orangery is the flagship restaurant at the North's only five red star hotel, golf and spa resort, Rockliffe Hall. This 4 AA Rosette restaurant it headed up by executive chef, Richard Allen, one of the UK's most celebrated chefs with two of the highest industry accolades to his name - the Cateys' Head Chef of the Year and the Craft Guild of Chefs' Restaurant Chef of the Year.

The Orangery restaurant offers an unrivalled dining experience, garden-to-plate ethos and exceptional wine pairings from some of the world's most exquisite vineyards, expertly selected by Rockliffe Hall's head sommelier, Daniel Jonberger.

Many of the dishes you will enjoy in The Orangery use ingredients foraged from the Rockliffe estate or grown within the resort's kitchen garden. Each night Richard takes guests on a unique food journey with his carefully crafted à la carte and tasting menu experiences. He's won many awards since joining Rockliffe Hall and most notably featured in the Sunday Times Top 100 Restaurants.

The restaurant is located in the 18th Century Old Hall building at Rockliffe Hall which boasts attractive original features including the Old Hall Arches and of course the beautiful, light and airy Orangery. For those wanting to stay a while, the hotel, which won Visit England's Large Hotel of the Year award, also has 61 stunning rooms, two additional restaurants, an award-winning spa and 18-hole Championship golf course.

The Orangery is the flagship 4 AA Rosette restaurant at Rockliffe Hall, offering exceptional food and drink and friendly, impeccable service at the North's only five red star resort.

ASPARAGUS WITH HARISSA

SERVES 4

🍷 *Luis Zebra, Granito Cru, Douro, 2016 (Portugal)*
A scintillating wine, at once fleshy and intensely mineral, with notes of citrus fruit, apricot and honey, as well as white pepper and curry spice. It has a marvellous twang of caramelised clementine in the background.

Ingredients

Harissa

300g deseeded chillies (chopped)
3 roasted red peppers (peeled, chopped)
3 tsp dry roasted cumin seeds
3 tsp dry roasted fennel seeds
3 tsp dry roasted coriander seeds
4 red onions (diced)
1 bulb garlic (crushed)
200ml tomato juice
½ litre good quality olive oil
1 lime (juice of)
salt and black pepper, to taste

Asparagus

1 bunch asparagus (peeled)
salt
olive oil (drizzle of)

Garnish

pine nuts (fried in smoked rapeseed oil and smoked salt)

Method

For The Harissa

Place the chillies, red peppers, spices, onions and garlic in a heavy-based pan and cook until all the moisture has gone and the ingredients start to stick to the pan. Add the tomato juice and reduce until dry. Remove the pan from the heat and leave to cool. When cold, place the mixture into a food processor and very slowly, while the blender is going, add the olive oil until the mixture *emulsifies* and creates a thick dressing consistency. Add a squeeze of lime and season to taste.

Transfer to a container, refrigerate and keep until needed.

> **Chef's Tip**
> This recipe will make more harissa than you need but it keeps well in the fridge.

For The Asparagus

Cook the asparagus in boiling, salted water for 20 seconds, then place in iced water. Strain, pat dry and set aside.

To Serve

Place the cooked asparagus in a dry frying pan on medium heat and warm gently, turning after about 1 minute. Season with salt and a drizzle of olive oil. Serve as pictured.

SQUAB PIGEON, CHERVIL ROOT DASHI, MUSHROOM KETCHUP

SERVES 4

Jiménez-Landi, 'Sotorrondero' Méntrida 2010 (Spain)
An intriguing blend of 80% Syrah, 15% Merlot and 5% Cabernet Sauvignon. The nose is very rich indeed but not at all heady. Sweet start and beautifully balanced. Lively follow-through and soft as anything at the end. The beautiful tannins are just teasing in the background.

Ingredients

Mushroom Ketchup

200g very fresh button mushrooms (thoroughly cleaned)
40g oyster sauce
1 tsp rice wine vinegar
salt (to taste)
1g xanthan gum

Vegetables

4 large chervil roots (washed)
smoked rapeseed oil (drizzle of)
salt (pinch of)
2 small heads hen of the woods mushrooms
4 young leeks

Duck Yolks

4 duck eggs (separated)

Pigeon And Dashi

2 squab pigeons
salt (to taste)
vegetable trimmings
2 shallots (peeled, sliced)
1 clove garlic (peeled, crushed)
2 pieces kelp
2 litres vegetable stock
smoked rapeseed oil (drizzle of)

To Serve

250g unsalted butter (diced)
black truffle (well-scrubbed)

Method

For The Mushroom Ketchup

Blend the mushrooms in a processor, then pass the liquid through double muslin cloth. Add the oyster sauce, rice wine vinegar and salt to taste, then blend in the xanthan gum.

For The Vegetables

Trim both ends of the chervil roots. Keep the trimmings. Vac pack the roots with the rapeseed oil and salt. Place in a steamer at 80°C for 2 hours, until tender. Leave in the bag and chill in an ice bath.

Split the mushroom clumps into 4, remove any dirt or bad areas. Trim the base, keep the trimmings.

Wash the leeks well, especially the roots. Peel the first layer, trimming as necessary. *Blanch* in boiling, salted water for 2 minutes, refresh and reserve. Keep the trimmings.

For The Duck Yolks

Vac pack the yolks, season and cook in a water bath at 60°C for 2 hours. Remove and blend until smooth.

For The Pigeon And Dashi

Preheat the oven to 165°C (fan).

Remove the legs, wings and breasts from the pigeons, take out the innards and discard, reserve the hearts.

Roast the crowns for 45 minutes, then set aside.

Place the legs and wings in a hot, heavy-based pan and brown on a high heat. Add salt and the vegetable trimmings along with the shallots and garlic. Sweat for 2 minutes continuously stirring. Add the kelp, stock, pigeon crowns and hearts. Simmer for 45-60 minutes, skim as necessary. Pass the stock through double muslin and season. Keep hot.

Remove the skin and sinew from each pigeon breast, vac pack with a drizzle of smoked rapeseed oil and salt, set aside.

To Assemble The Dish

Place the pigeon breasts in a water bath at 60°C for 9 minutes.

Cut the chervil roots in half and brown in hot, foaming butter. Remove and strain. Cut the *blanched* leeks into 4, then char directly on the stove top for a few seconds.

Put 1 teaspoon of egg yolk and 1 of ketchup in the bottom of each serving bowl. Add the hot, browned chervil and charred leek evenly into each bowl. Char the cooked pigeon on the stove top. Cut each breast into 4 and arrange in the bowls. Grate over the fresh black truffle. Finally, add the hot dashi at the table.

GARIGUETTE STRAWBERRY, ESTATE FENNEL

SERVES 4

🍷 *Late Harvest Sauvignon Blanc Eradus 2017,
Marlborough, South Island (New Zealand)
Appealing aromas of apricots, dried fruit and
honey on the nose. The palate shows mango,
tropical fruit and melon flavours and great limey
acidity which gives backbone to the ripe fruit.
A lingering, delicious finish!*

Ingredients

Strawberry Purée

500g fresh strawberries (hulled, chopped)
120g jam sugar

Strawberry Custard

75g sugar
90g egg yolks
120g whole eggs
350g strawberry purée
50ml whipping cream
20ml white balsamic
3 leaves gelatine (soaked in cold water)

Crumble

60g butter
60g sugar
120g plain flour

Sponge

120g egg whites
80g egg yolks
80g sugar
25g plain flour
10g fennel pollen

Fennel Meringue

30g sugar
30g albumen powder
5g fennel pollen
10ml sambuca

Garnish

8 Gariguette strawberries
1 punnet fennel shoots

4 large, disposable coffee cups (greased, holes pierced in the base)

Method

For The Strawberry Purée

Combine the ingredients and cook gently until the sugar has dissolved. Simmer for 1½ hours, then blend, chill and reserve.

For The Strawberry Custard

Whisk the sugar and eggs until white. Add the strawberry purée and whipping cream and cook in a heavy-based saucepan on a low heat, continuously stirring, until the mix reaches 80°C. While hot, stir in the balsamic vinegar and gelatine leaves. Chill and reserve.

For The Crumble

Preheat the oven to 165°C (fan).

Rub the ingredients together to a sandy texture. Cook until golden, about 15-20 minutes, then cool on the tray and set aside.

For The Sponge

Blend all the ingredients in a food processor, then transfer to a cream whipper and charge it with 2 gas bulbs. Leave to stand for 20 minutes. Spray the mix into the greased coffee cups, before microwaving for 20 seconds. Leave to cool in the cups.

Alternatively, bake the cake in the traditional way; same ingredients and quantities, bake in a small cake tin (165°C fan) until firm in the centre.

For The Fennel Meringue (Prepare ahead)

Preheat the oven to its lowest setting.

Whisk the ingredients until firm peaks, then pipe onto a non-stick sheet. Dry in the oven overnight or until crisp. Transfer to an airtight container.

To Serve

Serve as pictured.

Chef's Tip

Balsamic vinegar and black pepper enhance the flavour of the strawberry perfectly. Add a small touch of one, or both, depending on taste, before serving.

152
PEACE & LOAF

217 Jesmond Road, Newcastle upon Tyne, NE2 1LA

0191 281 5222
www.peaceandloaf.co.uk Instagram: peaceandloafjes

Having opened its doors to the public in Autumn 2013, Peace & Loaf has earned its reputation of being on the culinary compass of any food connoisseur, both from inside and outside of the region.

Run and owned by David Coulson, who was a finalist of 2010 MasterChef, the Professionals, Peace & Loaf offers its diners exciting, seasonal menus.

For the last six years, David's signature dishes have headed up the kitchen in this fine dining restaurant, minus a pretentious atmosphere.

David uses only the freshest, locally sourced produce to create dishes with his own inventive flare and signature style.

"Peace & Loaf makes eating out an adventure. But that doesn't mean it is not serious about serving good food." - Jay Rayner - Observer newspaper is just one of the quotes from respected critics over the years.

The fine dining restaurant has already won an endless array of awards for its cuisine, service and venue, appearing in the Michelin Guide and voted Best Local Restaurant in the North East, 2018 in the Waitrose Good Food Guide.

The restaurant offers such a diverse range of excellent dishes to wow their diners, with David's unrivalled reputation and passion for creating flavoursome and innovative dishes. Peace & Loaf has truly excited and intrigued even the most discerning of palates.

With a talented team behind him, David has created a destination venue to be proud of and one that is definitely on the culinary map as the place to visit in the region.

Recent awards: Top 100 Restaurants, Open Table. Best Restaurant, Observer Food Monthly. Finalist, North East Restaurant of the Year, Food Awards England, 2018.

TORCHED MACKEREL, BLOOD ORANGE, CARROT, COASTAL HERBS

SERVES 4

 René Muré Pinot Gris, Alsace, 2016
(France)

Ingredients

Mackerel
2 whole dayboat mackerels
Maldon sea salt (pinch of)
10ml rapeseed oil

Blood Orange Gel
100ml blood orange juice
25g Ultratex

Blood Orange Garnish
1 blood orange
white balsamic vinegar (splash of)

Carrot Garnish
2 carrots (peeled)
1 sprig thyme
butter (knob of)

Coastal Herb Garnish
oyster leaf
sea aster
coltsfoot

Method

For The Mackerel
Remove the fillets from the mackerel, then cut off the thin membrane and pin bone the fillets. Lightly score the skin of the mackerel to allow even cooking. Season with salt and lightly blow torch until just cooked. Leave to rest for 2 minutes. Season again with the rapeseed oil.

Chef's Tip
Always remove the membrane from mackerel before blow torching as it relaxes the flesh and prevents curling. It also ensures even cooking throughout.

For The Blood Orange Gel
Blitz the juice and Ultratex in a high-powered blender to a smooth gel. Reserve in a bottle.

For The Blood Orange Garnish
Remove the skin of the orange using a peeler. This will ensure only the very zest is taken. *Julienne* the zest as thinly as possible, then *blanch* 3 times in boiling water. This will tone down any bitterness. Compress the zest with the vinegar in a vac pack bag. Remove the bitter white pith of the orange. Cut the orange into segments, then halve.

For The Carrot Garnish
Slice one carrot 1mm thin using a mandoline. Place the raw carrot discs in salted iced water.

Place the other carrot in a vac pack bag with the thyme and butter and steam at 82°C for 11 minutes. Remove from the bag and cut into pound coin sized shapes.

To Serve
Serve as pictured garnished with the coastal herbs.

RACK OF LAMB, WHITE ASPARAGUS, RAZOR CLAM, WILD GARLIC

SERVES 5

 Alighieri Possessioni Rosso del Veronese, Veneto, 2016 (Italy)

Ingredients

Lamb
1 whole saddle of lamb
2 sprigs thyme
salt and pepper

White Asparagus
1 bunch white asparagus (cleaned)
butter (knob of)
water (splash of)
wild garlic powder
sea salt

Lamb Jus
reserved lamb bones
mirepoix of vegetables
water (to cover)

Razor Clams
2 razor clams
200ml dashi
100ml lamb jus

Potatoes
4 potatoes (peeled, quartered)
250g butter
1 litre whole milk
salt

Garnish
wild garlic (chopped)

Method

For The Lamb Belly (Prepare ahead)
Vac pack the lamb belly with the thyme and steam overnight at 72°C. Remove the rib bones and membrane, then rebuild into a lamb belly shape and press overnight. Cut into 4-5cm portions. Gently reheat prior to serving.

For The Rack Of Lamb
Preheat the oven to 180°C (fan).

Trim the lamb rack, then *French trim* the rib bones. Remove the top layer of membrane and lightly score the fat.

Cook the rack, fat-side down, in a heavy-based pan and slowly render the fat for around 6 minutes until crisp and golden. Season, then transfer to the oven for 5-6 minutes (medium). Allow the lamb to rest for 6 minutes before carving the rack.

For The White Asparagus
Remove any hard stalks from the asparagus. Combine the butter and water in a pan to make an *emulsion*. When boiling hot, add the asparagus and cook for 2-3 minutes. Season with wild garlic powder and sea salt.

For The Lamb Jus (Prepare ahead)
Preheat the oven to 180°C (fan).

Roast the bones until brown, about 40 minutes. Transfer to a pan with the vegetables and water. Simmer for 2 hours. Strain, then reduce to 100ml.

For The Razor Clams
Gently cook the razor clams in the dashi, then leave them to cool in the liquid.

When ready to serve, drain the clams then slice them. Gently reheat the *jus* and add the razor clams.

> **Chef's Tip**
> Cooking the razor clams in dashi (seaweed stock) helps them to stay tender and it retains the natural sweet and salt flavour of the clams.

For The Potatoes
Boil the potatoes in salted water for 10-15 minutes until soft enough to mash. Drain the water off, then pass the potatoes through a ricer. Bring the butter and milk to the boil and combine with the mashed potato. Season with salt.

To Serve
Serve as pictured.

FOREST FLOOR, CHERRY, PISTACHIO, ITAKUJA

SERVES 4

🍷 *Pineau des Charentes Rouge 5 Years Old,*
Château de Beaulon Cognac (France)

Ingredients

Itakuja Chocolate Crémeux

110g egg yolk
200g caster sugar
500ml double cream, 500ml whole milk
700g Itakuja chocolate

Pistachio Micro Sponge

150g pistachio paste
70ml stock syrup, 180g egg whites
60g ground almonds

Kirsch Gel

250g sugar, 500ml vinegar
1 litre water, 200ml kirsch
6g agar agar

Pistachio Tuile

200g sugar, 40g plain flour
30g pistachio powder
2g salt, 100ml whole milk
140g butter (melted)
100g pistachios (chopped)

Chocolate Soil

100g sugar
100g ground almonds
60g plain flour
44g cocoa powder, 6g salt
70g butter (melted)

Green Tea Moss

25g sugar
25g unsalted butter
25g plain flour
25g ground almonds
7½g matcha powder

Garnish

edible petals

baking tray (lined)

Method

For The Itakuja Chocolate Crémeux

Place all the ingredients, except the chocolate, into a Thermomix set to 90°C and cook for 8 minutes. Add the chocolate and cook for a further 2 minutes. Chill until set. Alternatively, whisk the yolks and sugar in a large bowl. Gently heat the milk and cream to just below boiling, then gradually pour the hot milk mixture into the yolks, whisking constantly. When fully incorporated, stir in the chocolate. Chill until set.

For The Pistachio Micro Sponge

Combine all the ingredients in a blender, then transfer to an Isi gun, 2 charges. Alternatively, use a basic pistachio sponge recipe and dehydrate in a low oven overnight.

> **Chef's Tip**
> For an added crispy texture caramelise and dehydrate the micro sponge by placing it in the oven or dehydrator overnight at 70°C (fan).

For The Kirsch Gel

Bring the sugar, vinegar and water to the boil, then reduce to 400ml. Add the kirsch and stock syrup, then return to the boil with the agar agar. Blend in a powerful blender, then pass through a sieve to form a smooth gel.

For The Pistachio Tuile

Preheat the oven to 170°C (fan).
Sift the sugar, flour, pistachio powder and salt. Mix in the milk, then add the butter to form a paste. Stir in the chopped pistachios. Leave to set, then spread on a silicone mat and bake for 7 minutes.

For The Chocolate Soil

Preheat the oven to 170°C (fan).
Sift the sugar, ground almonds, flour, cocoa powder and salt into a mixing bowl, mix with the paddle attachment. Slowly pour in the melted butter, while mixing, until it looks like soil. Pour onto a lined baking tray and bake for 30 minutes, stirring every 10 minutes.

For The Green Tea Moss

Preheat the oven to 120°C (fan).
Cream the sugar and butter, fold through the flour and almonds, then mix in the matcha powder. Roll the paste into a log. Wrap in cling film and freeze. Use a microplane to grate the frozen green tea paste onto a silicone mat. Bake for 8 minutes.

To Serve

Serve as pictured, garnished with edible petals.

162
THE PIPE & GLASS

West End, South Dalton, East Yorkshire, HU17 7PN

01430 810 246
www.pipeandglass.co.uk Twitter: @pipeandglass Instagram: @pipeandglass Facebook: @pipeandglass

There are many reasons why The Pipe and Glass at South Dalton holds a coveted Michelin star.

Guests receive a warm welcome from James and Kate Mackenzie and team (he's the chef; she runs front of house), the atmosphere is inviting, unpretentious and relaxed; cool and airy in the summer, yet cosy and cocooning in colder weather. The real star of the show, of course, is the food, which has the top restaurant critics drooling. Jay Rayner in The Observer called The Pipe a "class act... there was no doubting the quality of the cookery", while The Independent's Christopher Hirst praised the "inventive Mackenzie" for "ingenious dishes" and for "not forgetting that he's running a pub."

The bar has kept a country pub feel alongside the elegant, airy restaurant and conservatory which looks out over the garden. The picturesque grounds include a kitchen garden and herbarium, which supply the restaurant, as well as two relaxed outdoor dining spaces.

Guests looking for something extra special can book the conservatory for parties of 20 or more or, even more exclusively, The Pipe's first-floor private dining room, the Hotham Room, for between six and ten people. For really luxurious overnight accommodation, there are The Pipe's boutique rooms, offering comfort and glamour.

Set in the glorious surroundings of the Hotham Estate, The Pipe and Glass holds East Yorkshire's first and only Michelin star and has previously held the title of Michelin Pub of the Year.

CRAB, CARROT AND CORIANDER SALAD, TOASTED HAZELNUTS, SEA SALT FLATBREAD

SERVES 4

 Unwooded Chardonnay, Pitchfork
(Australia)

Ingredients

Crab, Carrot And Coriander Salad

½ cucumber
1 green chilli
500g fresh white crab meat
1 tbsp crème fraîche
2 limes (juice of)
1 bunch fresh coriander (chopped)
salt and pepper
3 carrots (coloured if possible)
1 tbsp rapeseed oil

Sea Salt Flatbreads

10g fresh yeast
90ml tepid water
5g salt
5g sugar
25ml olive oil
210g strong plain flour
10g Parmesan (grated)
10g sea salt

Toasted Hazelnuts

80g hazelnuts (shelled)

Garnish

1 punnet micro coriander

Method

For The Crab, Carrot And Coriander Salad

Cut the cucumber in half lengthways, remove the seeds and dice. De-seed and finely chop the chilli. Place the cucumber and chilli in a mixing bowl with the crab meat, crème fraîche, the zest and juice of 1 lime and half the coriander. Mix and season with salt and pepper, cover and store in the fridge until needed.

Peel the carrots and cut on a spiralizer to form a 'spaghetti' of carrot. Place in a bowl with the rest of the chopped coriander, juice of 1 lime, rapeseed oil and a good pinch of salt. Leave to marinate in the fridge for up to 30 minutes.

For The Sea Salt Flatbreads

Dissolve the yeast in the tepid water, add all the other ingredients to a mixing bowl and pour in the water. Mix to a dough and knead until smooth. You can do this in a mixer with the dough hook or a food processor. Place into a bowl, cover with cling film and leave to prove in a warm place until doubled in size.

Preheat the oven to 160°C (fan).

Place the dough onto a lightly floured surface and knock back. Divide the dough into 4 equal balls. Roll through a pasta machine to the number 2 setting, lay the sheets out and cut into triangles. Lay the triangles onto a non-stick baking sheet, brush with some olive oil, sprinkle with some sea salt flakes and bake for a few minutes until crisp.

For The Toasted Hazelnuts

Toast the hazelnuts in a dry frying pan or under a hot grill, remove any skins by rubbing in a clean tea towel. Roughly chop.

To Serve

Place a large cutter in the middle of the plate, spoon some of the crab mixture into the ring and lightly press down. Take the carrot mix and place on top of the crab mix. Dress with the hazelnuts, micro coriander and some of the carrot marinade.

Chef's Tip

We also garnish this dish with a carrot and orange gel, coriander mayonnaise and thickened lemon purée.

SALT BEEF HASH CAKE, FRIED QUAIL EGG, RHUBARB KETCHUP, PICKLED ONION RINGS

SERVES 4

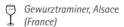

Gewurztraminer, Alsace (France)

Ingredients

Salt Beef Hash Cakes

½ large white onion (peeled, fine diced)
oil (drizzle of)
1 tsp chopped fresh thyme
black pepper and sea salt
200g dry mashed potato
2 spring onions (thinly sliced)
½ bunch fresh chives (chopped)
½ bunch flat leaf parsley (chopped)
1 tbsp grain mustard
200g cooked salt beef
rapeseed oil (for frying)
butter (large knob of)

Rhubarb Ketchup

200g Yorkshire rhubarb
½ large white onion (peeled, chopped)
100g caster sugar
100g dark brown sugar
200ml cider vinegar
¼ tsp ground mixed spice
1 star anise
Worcestershire sauce (dash of)
½ clove garlic

Pickled Onion Rings

2 large pickled onions
100ml whole milk
100g gluten free plain flour
rapeseed oil (for frying)
salt (pinch of)

To Serve

4 quail eggs
rapeseed oil (drizzle of)
butter (knob of)
chervil

Method

For The Salt Beef Hash Cakes

Place the onion into a frying pan with a drop of oil, the thyme and a touch of salt and pepper. Fry the onions until soft and translucent, remove from the heat and cool.

Place the mashed potato in a mixing bowl, drain any liquid off the sweated onion and add to the mash with the herbs, spring onions and mustard.

Chop the beef into 2cm size strips and add to the mash. Mix all together and season with some black pepper and a little salt, if needed. Divide the mix into 4 and make into cakes using a large round cutter with a dusting of flour, if required. They should be big enough to sit the fried egg on top. Place them on a tray and refrigerate until required.

For The Rhubarb Ketchup

Place all the ingredients in a large saucepan. Bring to the boil and simmer until the rhubarb becomes a shiny chutney consistency. Remove the star anise then blitz with a stick blender. Pass the cooked rhubarb through a sieve. Reduce a little more if required. Pour the ketchup into a squeezy bottle and refrigerate until cold.

For The Pickled Onion Rings

Thinly slice the pickled onions and pass the outer onion rings through milk and flour. Dust off the excess flour and repeat the process again. Deep fry the rings in hot oil (180°C) until golden and crispy. Remove from the fryer, place onto kitchen paper and sprinkle with a little salt.

To Serve

Shallow fry the hash cakes in some rapeseed oil and a good knob of butter, cook for about 4 minutes on each side until golden brown. Fry the eggs in a little rapeseed oil and a knob of butter, place the egg on top of the cake in the centre of a plate. Garnish with blobs of the rhubarb ketchup, pickled onion rings and the chervil.

> **Chef's Tip**
>
> Crisp pickled onion rings are great served as a canapé or accompaniment to beer. The ketchup also complements grilled mackerel well and, as an alternative, can be made using gooseberries instead of rhubarb.

DARK CHOCOLATE HONEYCOMB BITES

MAKES 30 BITES

*Pedro Ximénez
(Spain)*

Ingredients

Dark Chocolate Honeycomb Bites

75g honey
540g sugar
5 tbsp water
20g bicarbonate of soda
300g good quality dark chocolate buttons
(54% minimum)

large tray (lined with greaseproof paper)
silicone mat

Method

To Make The Dark Chocolate Honeycomb Bites

Put the honey, sugar and water into a deep pan (it needs to be deep as the mix will bubble up to the top) and bring to the boil. Continue boiling until the mix turns light golden in colour. Remove from the heat and immediately whisk in the bicarbonate of soda - this is when the mix will really bubble up. Pour onto the prepared tray and allow to cool. When cool, break into bite-sized pieces by tapping with the heel of a knife.

Melt 200g of the chocolate in a bowl over a pan of hot water. Remove from the heat and add the other 100g of chocolate, stir to melt. While the chocolate is still runny, dip and coat the pieces of honeycomb in it, then lay onto some greaseproof paper or a silicone mat and allow to set.

At the Pipe and Glass we serve these as a garnish with our cinder toffee ice cream, which has been on the menu since day one and is always a firm favourite with our customers!

Chef's Tip

When the mix turns light golden in colour, speed is of the essence; remove from the heat immediately and add the bicarbonate to prevent overcooking.

172
THE ROSE & CROWN AT ROMALDKIRK

Barnard Castle, County Durham, DL12 9EB

01833 650 213
www.rose-and-crown.co.uk Twitter: @therandc Facebook: roseandcrownhotel

Since taking over the Rose & Crown in 2012, Thomas and Cheryl Robinson have invested heavily in bringing this well-known hostelry up-to-date and, in the early months of 2018, this included a brand new kitchen for the skilled team of chefs led by Dave Hunter, who has returned to head up the kitchen after a year in a 2 Michelin star establishment.

This quintessential Dales inn dates back to the mid 18th Century and its fabulous heritage stands out as soon as you walk through the front door. The period charm has been blended with relaxed and authentic interior design; from the bar with its stone flagged floors, open fireplace and bespoke English-made furniture to the lovely oak panelled restaurant and the 14 stylish guest bedrooms beyond.

The food strikes a balance between inventive yet hearty pub favourites and more fine dining dishes that showcase an excellent understanding and knowledge of contemporary British cooking. A focus on ingredients with strong provenance and local relevance is at the forefront of the menu as is a passion for high standards of animal welfare. Whether celebrating a special occasion in the restaurant or just enjoying a bite to eat in the bar with the dog under the table, the Rose & Crown is a very welcoming place to be.

DOG TREATS
(HELP YOURSELF)

Dave Hunter is a chef who lives and breathes cooking, having both an amazing knowledge of his profession and a genuine passion for his native North East... and Liverpool FC!

TEMPURA MONKFISH WITH VADOUVAN SPICE, MUSHY PEAS, TARTARE SAUCE HOLLANDAISE

SERVES 4

 Viognier 2017 Moulin de Gassac, D`Oc, Languedoc (France)

Ingredients

Mushy Peas

115g dried marrowfat peas
1 tbsp bicarbonate of soda
150ml cold water
salt and pepper (to season)

Tartare Hollandaise

150g unsalted butter
2 large free-range egg yolks
1 dtsp white wine vinegar
20g shallot (finely diced, *sautéed*)
20g gherkin (finely diced)
20g capers (finely diced)
20g parsley (finely chopped)
sea salt (to season)
1 lemon (spritz of)

Tempura Batter

100g cornflour
150g plain flour
10g baking powder
iced soda water (as required)

Monkfish

4 x 100g monkfish pieces (skinned, membrane removed)
plain flour (to dust)
oil (to deep fry)
20g good quality vadouvan spice
salt (to season)

Method

For The Mushy Peas (Prepare ahead)

Soak the peas in cold water with the bicarbonate of soda overnight.

Wash the peas and cover barely with clean water. Cook until soft and mushy. Blend until smooth, then season.

For The Tartare Hollandaise

Half fill a saucepan with water and bring to a simmer. Turn down the heat to as low as it can go but still have the water just simmering.

Melt the butter over a low heat until fully melted, then remove from the heat.

Place the egg yolks in a heatproof mixing bowl which will sit stably on the saucepan of water. Place the bowl on the pan. It is important that the saucepan is on a low heat, or the eggs will scramble.

Using a balloon whisk, start to beat the eggs, then whisk in the vinegar. Keep whisking, then start adding the melted butter by slowly drizzling it in, whisking all the time, until all the butter has been incorporated. The result should be a lovely, smooth, thick sauce. Add the diced ingredients. Season carefully with sea salt and loosen, if necessary, with little squeezes of lemon juice.

For The Tempura Batter

Combine the dry ingredients, then add enough iced soda water to make a batter that can coat your finger.

> **Chef's Tip**
> Whisk plenty of air into the batter for a lighter finish.

For The Monkfish

Dredge the monkfish in flour and tap off the excess. Dip in the tempura batter, then deep fry (180°C) for 5-6 minutes until golden. Drain on kitchen paper, then season with salt and a generous sprinkling of vadouvan spice.

To Serve

Serve as pictured.

BUTTER POACHED FILLET OF JOE SIMPSON'S BEEF, ROAST BONE MARROW, CRISPY TONGUE, BRAISED OX CHEEK

SERVES 4

 Malbec Single Vineyard Los Miradores 2014 Luigi Bosca, Mendoza (Argentina)

Ingredients

Ox Cheek And Crispy Tongue

2 carrots (diced)
2 onions (diced)
oil (drizzle of)
2 ox cheeks
1 sprig thyme
1 bay leaf
200ml red wine
1 ox tongue

Joe Simpson's Beef Fillet

500g butter
2 x 340g pieces top quality beef fillet
salt and pepper

Roast Bone Marrow

2 x 12cm pieces bone marrow (split lengthways)
salt and pepper
2 slices white bread (made into breadcrumbs)
50g parsley (chopped)

To Serve

roast potatoes
baby vegetables

Method

For The Ox Cheek And Crispy Tongue (Prepare ahead)

Preheat the oven to 150°C (fan).

Sauté the carrots and onions in the oil in a large pan until soft and lightly golden. Remove the vegetables, heat a little more oil and seal the ox cheeks on all sides. Return the vegetables to the pan, add the herbs and *deglaze* with the red wine. Place the tongue in the pan and cover with water. Cook in the oven for 3-4 hours until soft then leave to cool. Remove the meat from the cooking liquid, then strain the liquid into a clean pan and reduce to a sauce consistency.

Peel the tongue and cut into large dice. Cut the ox cheek into 4 equal portions. Pan fry the tongue until crispy. Heat the cheek up in the sauce.

For Joe Simpson's Beef Fillet

Melt the butter in a deep pan big enough to hold the beef. Heat to 55°C holding it at that temperature. Cook the beef for 45 minutes.

Heat a cast iron frying pan until hot. Seal the fillet on all sides then leave to rest for 5-7 minutes.

> **Chef's Tip**
>
> Ask your butcher to trim the beef fillet for you. We have used our quality butcher Joe Simpson for over 25 years; he has his own animals and his own abattoir.

For The Roast Bone Marrow

Preheat the oven to 180°C (fan).

Season the bone marrow and roast in the oven for 12 minutes until soft.

Combine the breadcrumbs and parsley, then top the bone marrow with the mix. Cook for a further 2 minutes.

To Serve

Serve as pictured with roast potatoes and baby vegetables.

CHOCOLATE FALCON, PISTACHIO, BLACKBERRY

SERVES 8

🍷 *Elysium Black Muscat 2016, Andrew Quady, California (USA)*

Ingredients

Tempered Chocolate Case

400g dark chocolate pistols (67%)

Chocolate Crémeux Filling

175ml double cream
40g egg yolk
20g caster sugar
100g dark chocolate (above 63%)
100g milk chocolate
salt (pinch of)

Pistachio Ice Cream

125g unsalted pistachio nuts (shelled)
75g caster sugar
3 free-range egg yolks
500ml double cream

Pistachio Crumble

90g sugar
110g ground pistachios
95g self-raising flour
salt (pinch of)
60g butter (melted)

To Serve

micro herbs
poached blackberries in blackberry jus

chocolate mould of your choice

Method

For The Tempered Chocolate Case

Place 300g of chocolate in a bowl and place over a *bain-marie*, slowly heating the water ensuring it does not boil. Stir the chocolate regularly using a flexible spatula so that it melts smoothly.

Check the temperature with a thermometer. When the chocolate reaches 55-58°C, remove the bowl from the *bain-marie*.

Add the remaining chocolate to the melted chocolate, stirring constantly. Stir until you reach a temperature of 28-29°C. Pour the melted chocolate into the mould and turn upside down to get rid of any excess chocolate. Leave to set.

> **Chef's Tip**
> Use the best quality chocolate you can afford.

For The Chocolate Crémeux Filling

Heat the cream to 80°C. Whisk the sugar and egg yolk together until light and fluffy. Mix the cream and egg yolk together and cook until the mixture coats the back of a spoon. Pour the cream mixture over both chocolates and stir until melted and glossy. Leave to cool slightly, then pour into the moulds. Leave to set, then unmould.

For The Pistachio Ice Cream (Prepare ahead)

Blend half the pistachios with half the sugar in a food processor until very fine. Roughly chop the remaining pistachios with a sharp knife on a secure chopping board.

Whisk the egg yolks with the remaining sugar in a large bowl until thick and creamy.

Place the cream and the pistachio/sugar mixture into a heavy-based pan over a medium heat and bring to the boil. Immediately remove from the heat and pour the mixture onto the egg yolks, whisking constantly. Return the pistachio custard to the pan and stir over a low heat until the mixture thickens. Refrigerate for at least 3 hours. Churn in an ice cream machine. Fold in the hand chopped pistachios. Freeze until required.

For The Pistachio Crumble

Preheat the oven to 160°C (fan).

Mix all the dry ingredients together, then add the melted butter, stirring until combined. Bake for 10 minutes, stir, then bake for another 10 minutes.

To Serve

Serve as pictured garnished with blackberries.

182
SHIBDEN MILL INN

Shibden Mill Fold, Shibden, Halifax, HX3 7UL

01422 365 840
www.shibdenmillinn.com Twitter: shibdenmill

Wind down the narrow country lanes of this lush West Yorkshire valley and stumble upon the family run Shibden Mill Inn. Picture a country inn and this place has it all, ancient beams and fireplaces, cosy nooks and crannies, a flower filled garden and buckets of character. It also boasts the warmest of welcomes and good old-fashioned hospitality.

This 17th Century building is a stunning backdrop for head chef Will Webster's very current dishes. With an eye for excellence and innovative food combinations, this young chef has passion and talent, creating imaginative dishes inspired by the seasons and fresh, local produce. Shibden Mill Inn has always been a favourite with 'foodies' and has held its 2 AA Rosette status for over ten years. Awarded the Good Pub Guides Yorkshire Dining Pub of the Year 2018/19 and Yorkshire's Favourite Pub 2018, it is obviously loved by locals. If you aren't lucky enough to live on the doorstep, stay over and enjoy its AA 5 Star Inn accommodation, leaving you free to sample the Cask Marque Ales and extensive wine list.

The Heaton family have been pouring heart and soul into this beautiful old building for over 20 years and it shows. Run with passion and creativity, you will be swept up in its charm.

By gum we love this place,
Best of Yorkshire.

KING SCALLOPS, CHICKEN SKIN CUSTARD, STRAWBERRIES, VER JUS, DUKKAH SPICE

SERVES 4

🍷 *Caparrone Pecorino, Colline Pescaresi, Contessa, Abruzzo (Italy)*

Ingredients

Chicken Skin Custard

8 medium eggs
200g chicken skin
300ml double cream

Ver Jus Gel

100ml ver jus
10g Ultratex

Dukkah Spice

1 tbsp hazelnuts
1 tbsp almonds
2 tbsp coriander seeds
2 tbsp cumin seeds
1 tbsp dried chickpeas
½ tbsp salt

Scallops

12 large king scallops
butter (knob of)

Garnish

strawberries (sliced)
10ml ver jus
micro coriander

Method

For The Chicken Skin Custard

Preheat the oven to 180°C (fan).

Place the chicken skin between 2 pieces of baking parchment and cook between 2 trays in the oven until crispy, about 30-40 minutes. Combine the cream, eggs and cooked chicken skin in a Thermomix, blend at 80°C until thick. Alternatively, heat all the ingredients in a pan over a low flame until thickened. Cool over ice while stirring every now and again. Blitz in a blender, season, then transfer to a piping bag for later.

> **Chef's Tip**
> Cool the custard as quickly as possible to avoid scrambling.

For The Ver Jus Gel

Whisk the Ultratex into the ver jus and keep whisking until a gel-like consistency.

For The Dukkah Spice

Toast the ingredients in a dry pan, then blend in a food processor to a coarse spice mix.

For The Scallops

Fry the scallops until golden, then flip over and baste with butter.

To Serve

Dress the strawberries in ver jus and garnish the dish with micro coriander.

STONE BASS, CARAMELISED CAULIFLOWER PUREE, ROASTED CAULIFLOWER, PARISIENNE POTATOES, SMOKED ALMONDS, PARMESAN FOAM

SERVES 4

🍷 *Albariño 'D Pedro' Bodega Adegas Galegas, Rias Baixas (Spain)*

Ingredients

Caramelised Cauliflower Purée

500g cauliflower florets
200ml vegetable stock
1 litre whole milk
1 tsp xanthan gum

Roasted Cauliflower

1 cauliflower (cut into florets)
10ml rapeseed oil

Parisienne Potatoes

4 Maris Piper potatoes (peeled)
100ml vegetable stock
1 clove garlic
2 sprigs thyme
100g butter

Parmesan Foam

500ml whole milk
50g Parmesan (grated)
salt and pepper (to season)
8g soy lecithin
1 tsp xanthan gum

Stone Bass

4 x 150g stone bass portions (skin on)
oil (drizzle of)

To Serve And Garnish

butter (large knob of)
smoked almonds
sea purslane

Method

For The Caramelised Cauliflower Purée

Fry off the florets until nicely caramelised, then *deglaze* the pan with the stock, scraping the bottom of the pan. Reduce the stock by half, then add the milk and simmer until the cauliflower is cooked. Blend the cauliflower with the xanthan gum in a little of the milk until smooth.

For The Roasted Cauliflower

Blanch the cauliflower in water until just undercooked, then cool under running water. Once cooled, halve the florets leaving a flat side for roasting and set aside.

For The Parisienne Potatoes

Cut out balls from the potatoes using a melon baller. Bring the vegetable stock up to the boil with the garlic and thyme and whisk in the cold butter. Season and add the potatoes until just cooked. Take out of the liquid and cool.

For The Parmesan Foam

Bring the milk and Parmesan up to the boil, then take off the heat. Season and add the other ingredients. Blend and set aside.

For The Stone Bass And To Serve

Preheat the oven to 180°C (fan).

Pan fry the bass, skin-side down, with a little oil for 1 minute, then add the cauliflower and roast in the oven for 6 minutes. Take out of the oven, add butter and rest in the warm butter, skin-side up. Gently warm the other elements. Garnish with sea purslane and smoked almonds. Finish by blending the warm foam and spoon over the top of the fish.

Chef's Tip

When reheating the Parmesan foam, don't exceed 60°C as it will not foam as well.

SHIBDEN'S SNICKERS

SERVES 4

 Champagne Vollereaux
(France)

Ingredients

Peanut Butter Parfait

75ml double cream
60g egg yolks
75g caster sugar
140ml water
50g smooth peanut butter
1 leaf gelatine (soaked in cold water)

Peanut Shortbread

30g icing sugar
45g plain flour
45g ground almonds
15g unsalted butter
65g peanut butter
8ml double cream

Salted Caramel

125g caster sugar
125ml water
125ml double cream
25g unsalted butter
salt (pinch of, to taste)

Chocolate Mousse

60g Callebaut dark chocolate (70.5%)
100ml double cream
25g whole egg
8g caster sugar
3ml water (to dissolve sugar)

Salted Caramel Ganache

115g white chocolate
100ml double cream
25g whole egg
8g dark soft brown sugar
3ml water (to dissolve sugar)

Chocolate Tuile

50g Trimoline
50g isomalt
50g Callebaut dark chocolate (70.5%)

4 individual parfait moulds

Method

For The Peanut Butter Parfait

Whip the cream to soft peaks and set aside. Whisk the egg yolks on high speed. Place the sugar and 40ml of the water into a pan and boil until 118°C. Add to the yolks in the mixer. Heat the peanut butter and remaining water, stir in the gelatine, then add this to the mixer. Mix until cool, then fold in the cream carefully. Set in moulds in the freezer.

For The Peanut Shortbread

Preheat the oven to 160°C (fan).

Add all the ingredients to a mixer and beat slowly until a dough consistency. Roll the dough to the thickness of a pound coin. Bake on a tray lined with baking parchment for 12-15 minutes. Cut out using a metal ring.

For The Salted Caramel

Boil the sugar and water to a caramel, then slowly whisk in the cream and bring back to the boil. Add the butter and salt, then leave to cool.

For The Chocolate Mousse

Melt the chocolate over a *bain-marie*. Lightly whip the cream to soft peaks. Begin whipping the eggs, then warm the sugar and water until fully dissolved. Pour onto the eggs while whisking, then fold in the melted chocolate and whipped cream. Store in a piping bag.

For The Salted Caramel Ganache

Melt the white chocolate over a *bain-marie*. Lightly whip the cream to soft peaks. Beat the eggs in a mixer, warm the sugar and water until boiling. Pour onto the eggs while whisking and whisk until cool. Fold through the white chocolate and cream and place in a piping bag.

For The Chocolate Tuile

Bring the isomalt and Trimoline up to the boil and heat to a light caramel. Add the chocolate and whisk until melted. Set on baking parchment, then pull while still a little warm.

To Serve

Assemble on a plate as pictured and top with the tuile.

Chef's Tip

Do not overcook the sugar, if you do, start again.
Be very careful not to overmix the caramel ganache, it splits very easily.

(see glossary)

192
THE VIOLET GREEN

68a The Green, Norton, TS20 1BN

01642 533 006
www.thevioletgreen.co.uk Instagram: the_violetgreen

Tucked in the basement of an old bank, The Violet Green, is the newest and very welcomed restaurant below Norton Green in Norton, a part of Stockton on Tees in Teesside. The relaxed and informal restaurant is owned and run by Anna and Chris Hand, with the restaurant being named after Anna's great grandmother.

The carefully chosen menus focus on local and seasonal produce. The fish comes from Hodgson's and all the meat is supplied by Anna's family butchers, Blackwell's of Norton. It really is a family butcher, having been passed down through the generations, with owner Anna now also running the butcher shop which was her father's and has been in the family for over 65 years.

Head chef Jack Butler is no stranger to Norton. A few years ago, he worked in Blackwell's, doing pop-ups, offering tasting menus, tapas nights and Sunday lunches. At that time, Anna and Chris, along with Jack, spoke of their mutual desire to open a restaurant.

Jack ventured further afield, gaining experience working as head chef in various locations however, he returned when The Violet Green was due to open.

"We all work closely together to provide a relaxed environment with informal, friendly service and refined, yet uncomplicated, food. We use local suppliers as much as possible but are not afraid to journey further afield if there is a better product out there," says Jack.

Recently, The Violet Green has been host to live music nights - 'Food, Booze and Blues', which is proving to be very popular - a perfect way to spend your evening.

A unique restaurant hidden
underneath Norton Green.

OCTOPUS, HOISIN PORK BELLY, PICKLED RHUBARB

SERVES 4

 Tombacco Pecorino (Italy)

Ingredients

Octopus
4 octopus tentacles
water (to cover)
salt

Pork Belly
300g pork belly
1 star anise
coriander seeds (pinch of)
fennel seeds (pinch of)
hoisin sauce

Pickled Rhubarb
1 stick forced Yorkshire rhubarb
60ml Chardonnay vinegar
40ml water
20g caster sugar •

To Serve
cashew nuts (roasted)
micro coriander

Method

For The Octopus (Prepare ahead)

Preheat the oven to 160°C (fan).

Place the octopus in a deep dish, cover in salted water, then cover with foil or with a lid. Braise the octopus for 1-1½ hours, or until a skewer goes easily through the thick end of the tentacle. Refrigerate until required.

For The Pork Belly

Preheat the oven to 170°C (fan).

Submerge the pork belly in water, then add the star anise, coriander and fennel seeds. Cover and cook for 1-1½ hours. Cool, then slice thinly.

For The Pickled Rhubarb (Prepare ahead)

Slice the rhubarb thinly, about 2mm, then place in a vac pack bag with the other ingredients. Seal in a vacuum chamber at least a day in advance. Alternatively, bring the vinegar, water and sugar to the boil, then chill. Drop in the rhubarb and leave for 2 hours.

To Serve

Start by heating 2 pans to a medium heat, add a splash of oil when hot. Season the octopus, then cook for 3 minutes on each side. Place on a draining tray to rest for a further 3 minutes.

Reheat the pork belly in the second pan over a low to medium heat, turning regularly until caramelised and golden. Leave to rest.

Brush the pork belly with the hoisin sauce, then arrange the pork and octopus on the plate as pictured. Top with cashew nuts and a generous amount of the pickled rhubarb. Garnish with coriander.

> **Chef's Tip**
> Don't be shy when caramelising the octopus.

FILLET OF BLACKWELL'S BEEF WITH HORNLEYS SAUCE

SERVES 4

 Plan B! Cabernet Sauvignon Sangiovese (Australia)

Ingredients

Chive Mash

4 Redskin potatoes (peeled)
120g butter
50ml double cream
chives (handful of, chopped)
salt

Carrot Purée

500g carrots (peeled, chopped)
700ml whole milk
50g butter

Hornleys Sauce

300g diced pancetta
20g green peppercorns
100ml brandy
1 litre beef stock
300g silverskin onions
10g chives
1 tbsp Worcestershire sauce

Beef Fillets

4 x 225g beef fillets
oil (drizzle of)
salt
2 cloves garlic
thyme (sprig of)
rosemary (sprig of)
60g butter

Broccoli Purée

1 head broccoli (florets of)
50g unsalted butter
salt (pinch of)
whole milk (splash of)

To Serve

12 spears Tender-stem broccoli

Method

For The Chive Mash

Cut the potatoes to even-sized dice, then place in a pan of cold water with a pinch of salt. Bring to the boil and cook until soft. Drain, then mash the potatoes. Return them to the pan, add the butter and a splash of double cream and mix well. Finish with chopped chives and salt to season.

For The Carrot Purée

Place the carrots in a pan and cover with milk. Bring to the boil and cook until soft, then sieve the carrots, reserving the milk. Blitz the carrots in a blender, then add the butter and a splash of the milk until you reach the desired texture. Pass the purée through a fine sieve, then taste and adjust the seasoning if needed.

For The Hornleys Sauce

Roast the pancetta in a pan until golden, then add the green peppercorns and *deglaze* with the brandy. Reduce the brandy down by at least two-thirds before adding the beef stock and bringing to a gentle simmer. Reduce the sauce until it coats the back of a spoon, then add the silverskin onions and cook for a further 4-5 minutes. Finish with chopped chives and a splash of Worcestershire sauce.

For The Beef Fillets

Preheat the oven to 190°C (fan).

Let the beef come to room temperature, then coat generously in salt and oil before bringing a pan to a high heat. Place the beef in the pan and sear on all sides until you have a deep golden colour all over the steak. Add the garlic and herbs to the pan and transfer to the oven for 4 minutes. Remove the beef from the pan and leave to rest for at least 5 minutes before slicing.

For The Broccoli Purée

Cook the florets in salted, boiling water until a knife can easily pass through, about 4-6 minutes. Strain, then blend with the butter and a pinch of salt. If the purée is too thick, add a splash of milk and continue to blend. Pass through a fine sieve and adjust seasoning.

> **Chef's Tip**
>
> Let your beef come to room temperature before cooking.

To Serve

Place the broccoli in a hot pan for 2 minutes each side until cooked through and charred. Slice the beef in half and serve as pictured.

PEANUT BUTTER MOUSSE, BANANA, RASPBERRY

SERVES 4

*Princess Butterfly Moscato
(Australia)*

Ingredients

Peanut Butter Mousse

300g smooth peanut butter
150ml whole milk
2½ leaves gelatine (soaked in cold water)
3 egg whites
60g caster sugar
200ml double cream

Banana Ice Cream

500ml whole milk
500g banana purée
60g caster sugar
6 egg yolks
100g ice cream stabiliser
55g gelatine

Raspberry Gel

300g raspberry purée
1-2 tsp Ultratex (or as required)

Garnish

1 banana
micro lemon balm
freeze-dried raspberries

4 x 7cm chefs rings

Method

For The Peanut Butter Mousse

Place the peanut butter and milk in a pan over a low heat. Stir continuously until they have incorporated, then add the gelatine. Whisk the egg whites until stiff peaks, then add the sugar until it is fully incorporated. Semi-whip the cream, then whisk the peanut butter with one-third of the cream until incorporated. Gently and slowly fold in the rest of the cream. Slowly fold in the meringue mix a little at a time. Pour into the moulds and set in the fridge for at least an hour.

Chef's Tip

Don't add the peanut butter too hot or it will split the mousse.

For The Banana Ice Cream

Place all the ingredients in a Thermomix and cook to 85°C on speed 5.5 for 7 minutes. Chill the mixture in the fridge until cold, then rest for a further hour. Churn in an ice cream machine, then freeze. Alternatively, make in the traditional method (see page 246).

For The Raspberry Gel

Blend the purée with the Ultratex until you reach your desired texture. If you make it too stiff, simply add a little water.

To Serve

Blow torch the outside of the mould to help release the mousse easily. Place on a plate and top with the raspberry gel and banana ice cream. Blow torch a chunk of banana with a dusting of caster sugar to caramelise and place next to the ice cream. Top with lemon balm and freeze-dried raspberries.

202
WALWICK HALL HOTEL & COUNTRY ESTATE

Walwick Hall, Humshaugh, Hexham, Northumberland, NE46 4BJ

01434 620 156
walwickhall.com Facebook: walwickhall Instagram: @walwickhall

Walwick Hall, a boutique country hotel and spa, is a place to unwind, a place to relax, a place to reconnect with your better self. A Grade II listed hall where history and heritage are subtly married to exceptional modern design detailing; creating a refined but unstuffy atmosphere of luxurious elegance.

Amid the magical, 100-acre Georgian landed estate are Chesters Stables, originating from 1891 but recently renovated to an exceptional standard offering a true, rural retreat. The seven self-catering stable suites offer style and luxury and incorporate many of the original features of the stables. With the addition of handmade kitchens, marble bathrooms, deep-pile carpets and toe-warming stoves, the one to four bedroomed stables offer a multitude of options, all with a distinctive contemporary spirit.

Two of the stable suites are even 'dog friendly' meaning you can bring ALL the family!

All this just a stone's throw away from Hexham. An unsurpassable home from home, which instantly transports you to a world away from the norm. There is only one Walwick.

Walwick delivers beautiful food alongside professional, yet relaxed and friendly service. Guests enjoy the tranquillity of the setting and the very best Northumberland has to offer.

POACHED ORGANIC SALMON & HERB BALLOTINE, SAFFRON MAYONNAISE, GRANOLA, CAPERBERRY

SERVES 4

 Alsace Pinot Gris (France) or Grüner Veltliner (Austria)

Ingredients

Poached Salmon And Herb Ballotine
600g organic salmon fillet (skinned)
table salt and ground black pepper
cayenne pepper (pinch of)
1 tbsp dill (chopped), 1 tbsp parsley (chopped)
1 leaf gelatine (soaked in cold water), 1 sheet nori

Cucumber, Fennel And Lime Salad
½ cucumber (peeled, seeds removed, thinly sliced)
1 fennel bulb (thinly shaved)
1 lime (juice and zest of), caster sugar (sprinkle of)

Red Tuile
40ml water, 15g T45 flour (plain flour)
10ml vegetable oil (plus extra for cooking)
2½ml red food colouring

Savoury Granola
25g oats, 1 tsp poppy seeds, 12g pine nuts
mixed spice (good pinch of)
8g peeled pistachio nuts, ½ tsp dark soy sauce
½ tsp onion jam, 25g honey
25g glucose, 20g sultanas, 14g apricots (chopped)
Maldon salt (good pinch of)
ground white pepper (pinch of)
10g black rice (shallow fried until crispy)
1 tsp sesame seeds
1 tsp fresh thyme leaves (chopped)

Saffron Mayonnaise
extra virgin olive oil (splash of)
saffron (pinch of), 100g mayonnaise
lemon juice (splash of)
ground white pepper and salt

Garnish
black caviar, caperberries
pea shoots, cherry tomato petal

Method

For The Poached Salmon And Herb Ballotine (Prepare ahead)

Cut the salmon fillet in half lengthways and place, what was the skin-side, up. Season, then sprinkle carefully with the cayenne and mixed herbs. Place the gelatine onto one side of the salmon, then carefully place the other length on top to make a 'salmon sandwich'. Lay the nori on the worktop and roll the salmon up in the nori. Firmly roll in cling film to completely encase the salmon.

Poach the salmon in slow simmering water for 4 minutes for every 225g of salmon. Using a temperature gauge, bring the core temperature to 42ºC. Once cooked, immediately place into iced water and leave for 10 minutes. Remove from the water and leave to rest for 24 hours.

For The Cucumber, Fennel And Lime Salad

Combine all the ingredients in a bowl and leave for 30 minutes before using.

For The Red Tuile

Mix all the ingredients together. Heat a frying pan with a touch of oil to a medium heat, add a little of the mixture and cook out until it stops bubbling and it dries out. Repeat. Leave to cool completely before using.

Savoury Granola

Preheat the oven to 160ºC (fan).

Toast the oats until golden brown.

Combine the poppy seeds, pine nuts, mixed spice and pistachios and roast for 5-7 minutes.

Gently heat the soy sauce, onion jam, honey and glucose, then combine all the ingredients together. Bake in the oven for 5 minutes, then allow to cool. Keep moving the mixture as it cools so it does not stick together.

For The Saffron Mayonnaise

Warm the olive oil, add the saffron, remove from the heat and leave to infuse and cool.

Mix in the mayonnaise and lemon juice, mixing well until fully incorporated. Season well.

To Serve

Serve as pictured.

ROAST HAUNCH OF VENISON, TEXTURES OF BEETROOT, KALE, BITTER CHOCOLATE SAUCE

SERVES 4

🍷 *Allendale Odessa Stout or Wylam 'Club of Slaughters' Stout (England)*

Ingredients

4 x 220g venison haunches

Rösti Potato
3 potatoes (peeled, grated, squeezed of excess liquid)
seasoning, 80g unsalted butter

Beetroot Gel
200ml beetroot juice
½g table salt, 25g veggie gel

Salt Baked Beetroot
2 large golden beetroot
2 large candy beetroot
2 large red beetroot
coarse sea salt, butter (large knob of)

Chocolate Jus
1 shallot (finely diced)
15g unsalted butter
1 clove garlic (crushed), 1 sprig thyme
½ tsp mixed green and pink peppercorns (crushed)
150ml red wine, 100ml beef stock
35g dark chocolate (70%)

Beetroot Crisps
2 large red beetroot (washed, peeled, thinly sliced)
oil (for frying)

Chocolate Tuile
140g potato (peeled, diced)
15g unsalted butter
½ tsp cocoa powder (to taste and colour as desired)
2 medium egg whites
table salt and freshly ground black pepper

To Serve
green kale (buttered)

blini pan
baking tray (lined with greaseproof paper)

Method

For The Rösti Potato
Preheat the oven to 180°C (fan).
Season the grated potato and mix well.
Heat a 4 small blini pan to medium heat. Place 10g of butter in each hollow. Split the potato between the blini hollows and press down firmly. Fry until golden brown on one side. Remove, then add another 10g of butter to each dent. Place the rösti back in, coloured-side up. Press down and fry until golden brown. Place the rösti on a tray and bake for 4 minutes in the oven. Cool on a wire rack. Reheat when needed if not using immediately.

For The Beetroot Gel
Whisk all the ingredients together. Place onto a medium heat and whisk until it comes to the boil. Transfer to a container and refrigerate until set. When set, blitz in a blender until smooth, then pass through a sieve.

For The Salt Baked Beetroot
Preheat the oven to 145°C (fan).
Place some of the salt in the bottom of a roasting tray, sit the beetroot on top keeping them separate, then cover in salt. Bake for 1½ hours or until tender. Cool, peel off the skin and quarter. Place in foaming butter, then transfer to the oven to reheat.

Chocolate Jus
Sauté the shallot in butter with the garlic, thyme and peppercorns until softened but not caramelised, about 4-5 minutes. Add the red wine and reduce until almost evaporated. Pour in the stock and reduce until thickened, about 10 minutes. Pass through a fine sieve. Reheat when ready to serve, whisking in the chocolate.

For The Beetroot Crisps
Lightly fry the beetroot slices in clean oil until crisp but not brown. Drain on kitchen paper and leave to cool.

For The Chocolate Tuile
Preheat the oven to 175°C (fan).
Place the potatoes into a pan of salted, boiling water and cook until tender. Drain, mash and leave to cool. Melt the butter and mix in the cocoa, then stir into the potatoes. When cool, stir in the egg whites and seasoning and mix well.
Spread out thinly with a palette knife onto the prepared tray and bake for 10-12 minutes until the potato turns golden brown.

For The Venison And To Serve
Place the venison into a hot pan, cook on one side for 3 minutes, turn over and cook for 2 minutes. Remove from the heat and rest for 5 minutes. Serve as pictured.

MILK CHOCOLATE & FIGS DACQUOISE

SERVES 8-10

🍷 *'Dundee Cake' Old Fashioned*
50ml dark spiced rum, 12½ml Amaretto, 12½ml
PX sherry, 4 dashes chocolate bitters. Stir all the
ingredients over ice, strain into a whisky tumbler,
fill with ice, garnish with an orange twist.

Ingredients

Milk Chocolate Ganache

200ml double cream
530g milk chocolate (chopped)
80g unsalted butter (diced)

Fig Iced Parfait

5 fresh figs
100g caster sugar
water (as required)
6 medium egg yolks
450ml double cream

Croustillant Feuilletine Praline

35g dark chocolate (70%)
250g hazelnut praline paste
130g feuilletine (fine dried French crêpes)
or cornflakes

Dacquoise Sponge

50g roasted hazelnuts
50g ground almonds
100g egg whites
105g caster sugar

Garnish

fresh figs (quartered)
chocolate sauce
toasted hazelnuts (crushed)

20cm square mould (lined with silicone paper)
baking tray (lined with parchment)

Method

For The Milk Chocolate Ganache (Prepare ahead)

Bring the double cream to the boil, then remove from the heat.
Add the chocolate to the hot cream along with the butter and stir
until melted. Pour the ganache into the prepared mould. Set
overnight in the fridge.

For The Fig Iced Parfait (Prepare ahead)

Halve the figs, scrape the seeds and pulp and discard the skins.
Place the sugar and enough water to cover it in a pan. Slowly
bring to the boil, then boil for 2 minutes. While the sugar is
cooking, place the yolks into an electric mixer and whisk on full
speed. Pour the sugar syrup over the egg yolks while the mixer is
still on. Keep whisking until it cools to room temperature. This is
called a pâté à bombe. Semi-whip the double cream, then
carefully fold into the pâté à bombe along with the fig pulp.
Do not overwhip. Pour the parfait into a deep plastic dish. Freeze
for 3 hours.

> **Chef's Tip**
> The fig iced parfait can be made well in advance with
> it being frozen.

For The Croustillant Feuilletine Praline

Melt the chocolate and praline paste in a *bain-marie*. When
melted, add the feuilletine or cornflakes to the mix. Roll the
croustillant between 2 sheets of baking parchment and leave
to set in the fridge for 45-60 minutes.

For The Dacquoise Sponge

Preheat the oven to 180°C (fan)

Blitz the hazelnuts with the almonds to a fine powder. Whip
the egg whites to soft peak, then add the caster sugar. Continue
to whisk for a couple of minutes to make a French meringue.
Carefully fold the nut powder into the meringue until well
combined, then spread evenly to 1cm thick on the baking tray
lined with parchment. Bake for 15 minutes.

To Assemble The Dacquoise

Stack the elements together, starting with the croustillant,
followed by the sponge, then the ganache. Cut into portions.
Dip into the toasted hazelnuts, then plate on a splatter of
chocolate sauce. Using an apple corer, cut long tubes of parfait
and stack on top of the ganache. Serve immediately.

212
THE WENSLEYDALE HEIFER HOTEL & RESTAURANT

West Witton, Leyburn, DL8 4LS

01969 622 322 www.wensleydaleheifer.co.uk
Twitter: @WensleyHeifer Facebook: The Wensleydale Heifer Instagram: thewensleydaleheiferofficial

Surrounded by spectacular North Yorkshire views and just a few miles from both Leyburn and Hawes, Dales boutique hotel, The Wensleydale Heifer, boasts top quality accommodation and dining which remains a firm favourite of locals and visitors alike.

The charming AA 5 star rated restaurant with rooms is led by father and son team Lewis and chef patron David Moss. The Heifer's wide-ranging menus showcase the very best in local produce both imaginatively and deliciously.

With a simple ethos of using only the best ingredients and letting them speak for themselves, David and head chef Craig Keenan's seriously tempting menu ranges from fabulous lobster and fresh fish, to stunning steaks, through to tapas dishes and some very posh and creative sandwiches for those looking for a lighter option. It goes without saying that the Sunday lunch boasts succulent meats, huge Yorkshire puddings and all the delicious trimmings you would expect.

All dishes are beautifully accompanied by the carefully selected beers and wines stocked by the Heifer and recommended by the extremely knowledgeable (and friendly!) sommelier Vince. Diners can choose to eat in the restaurant or the more casual settings of the Fish Bar or restaurant garden.

Guests who don't want to move can always treat themselves to an overnight stay in one of the Heifer's luxurious themed rooms and, of course, the Heifer's famous Yorkshire breakfast to round off the perfect stay.

Fresh, locally sourced and best quality ingredients, along with their in-house smokery, are the secret to the Heifer's consistently fantastic food. Coupled with an always warm welcome, it is perfect for a celebration or more relaxed meal for any occasion.

CHILLI SALT SQUID

SERVES 4

 Weinhaus Ress Riesling (Germany)
Crisp and dry with citrus notes

Ingredients

2 squid tubes (cut into rings, cleaned)

Chilli Flour

200g plain flour
2 tsp paprika
1 tsp chilli powder
1 tsp cayenne pepper
2 tsp salt

Som Tam Dressing

200g palm sugar
100ml water
100g tamarind paste
100ml fish sauce

Sweet Chilli Sauce

1kg caster sugar
½ litre cold water
100g glucose syrup
100ml white wine vinegar
4 chillies (roughly chopped)
2 sticks lemongrass (roasted, roughly chopped)
50g fresh ginger (roughly chopped)
4 cloves fresh garlic (peeled)
10g fresh basil
10g fresh coriander

Papaya Salad

50ml som tam dressing
birds eye chilli (freshly sliced, to taste)
1 clove garlic (thinly sliced)
50g green beans (cut into small batons)
6 cherry tomatoes (halved)
1 red chilli (cut into thin rings)
2 green papayas (peeled, *julienne*)
2 carrots (peeled, *julienne*)
20g toasted peanuts

Garnish

micro coriander or fresh coriander

Method

For The Chilli Flour

Place the ingredients into a mixing bowl and combine well. Set aside.

For The Som Tam Dressing

Place the palm sugar into a small saucepan with the water and put on a low heat. Dissolve the palm sugar but do not boil, this will take about 20 minutes. Add the tamarind and fish sauce, this will smell rather unpleasant but trust us, it is beautiful! Set aside.

For The Sweet Chilli Sauce

Combine the sugar, water and glucose in a large, heavy-based saucepan. Place on a high heat and bring to the boil. Reduce the heat and boil until a golden caramel is achieved. Remove from the heat and add the vinegar. Take care as the caramel will be very hot and will spit when the cool vinegar is added. Combine the vegetables and herbs in a bowl, then pour the hot caramel onto them. Leave to cool, but not in the fridge as the raw ingredients need to infuse the caramel. When completely cool, blend in a food processor until well broken up.

For The Papaya Salad

Place the som tam dressing in a mortar. Add birds eye chilli, as desired, and pound with the pestle to release the oils and heat from the chilli. Add the garlic, green beans, tomatoes and chilli. Continue to pound the raw ingredients to break them down slightly. Add a splash more dressing, then add the green papaya and carrot. Give another vigorous pounding, then add a splash more dressing to get everything well coated in the sweet and sour dressing. Finally, add the toasted peanuts and mix well.

For The Squid

Dip the squid rings into cold water, then into the chilli flour, giving them a good coating. Remove from the flour, then dip them back into the water, then back into the flour. The double dip method gives a light and crispy texture. Deep fry (180°C) for 2 minutes, drain onto kitchen paper and season.

To Serve

Place the squid rings in a bowl, take a handful of the salad and blot slightly on kitchen paper. Serve with a pot of fresh sweet chilli sauce and garnish with fresh coriander.

Chef's Tip

This recipe will make more sweet chilli sauce than you require however it keeps well in the fridge and is delicious with almost everything!

SEA BASS, WARM SALAD OF CHORIZO & NEW POTATOES

SERVES 4

*Chablis 1er Cru Montmains Jean-Marc Brocard
(France)*

Ingredients

Pesto

100g fresh basil
2 cloves garlic (crushed)
50g Parmesan (grated)
50ml olive oil
100ml vegetable oil
salt and pepper (to taste)
lemon (squeeze of)
25g pine nuts

Garlic Mayonnaise

2 free-range egg yolks
1 tsp white wine vinegar
1 heaped tsp mustard powder
300ml groundnut oil
2 cloves garlic (crushed)
flat leaf parsley (chopped, to taste)
1 lemon (juice of)
salt and pepper (to taste)

Warm Salad Of Chorizo And New Potatoes

olive oil (drizzle of)
12 new potatoes (cooked, halved)
200g small chorizo sausages (skinned, diced)
100g sun-blush tomatoes (drained)
50g fresh pesto
200g wild rocket
salt and pepper (to taste)

Sea Bass

2 large sea bass (scaled, deboned, cut into 4 fillets)
1 tbsp olive oil
salt and pepper
butter (knob of)

Garnish

pea shoots

Method

For The Pesto

Place all the ingredients into a food processor and blend until smooth.

For The Garlic Mayonnaise

Place the yolks into a round-bottomed bowl, add the vinegar and whisk vigorously. Whisk in the mustard powder, then start adding the groundnut oil, a tiny bit at a time, until it is all combined, ensuring the mix does not split and remains thick and creamy. Finally, add the garlic, parsley and lemon juice. Season with salt and pepper.

For The Warm Salad Of Chorizo And New Potatoes

Heat the oil in a large, hot frying pan, then add the potatoes, flat-side down, and begin to colour for about 2 minutes on a medium heat. Add the chorizo and fry lightly to release the oils. Turn the potatoes over and colour the other side, then add the tomatoes and pesto and give a good toss to incorporate the ingredients together. Remove from the heat and add the rocket to create a warm salad. Season with salt and pepper.

> **Chef's Tip**
>
> It is best to use a raw chorizo as it will yield more oil as the sausage cooks.

For The Sea Bass

Heat the oil over a medium heat in a large, non-stick frying pan. Season the fillets, then place into the pan, skin-side down. Turn the heat up slightly and continue to cook the fillets, skin-side down, for 80% of its cooking time, to ensure a crisp skin when serving. Flip the fillets over, turn the heat off, then add the butter. This will begin to foam and continue to cook the sea bass through.

To Serve

Assemble as pictured.

RHUBARB & CUSTARD PANNA COTTA, RHUBARB RIPPLE ICE CREAM

SERVES 4

 Tokaji Aszu 5 Puttonyos (Hungary)

Ingredients

Rhubarb

150g rhubarb
135g caster sugar
35ml water

Panna Cotta

350ml single cream, or whole/semi-skimmed milk
1 vanilla pod (scraped)
4 large egg yolks
100g caster or vanilla sugar
3 leaves gelatine (soaked in cold water for 10 minutes)

Rhubarb Ripple Ice Cream

250g fresh rhubarb (trimmed, sliced)
1 tbsp water
225g caster sugar
250ml double cream
250ml whole milk
1 vanilla pod (scraped)
4 medium eggs

Garnish

seasonal berries
micro coriander
rhubarb meringue

8 small ramekin dishes

Method

For The Rhubarb

Preheat the oven to 180°C (fan).

Combine the ingredients and bake on an oven tray for 20 minutes or until soft but not squidgy. Leave to cool.

For The Panna Cotta (Prepare ahead)

Gently bring the cream or milk with the vanilla pod and seeds to the boil.

In the meantime, whisk together the egg yolks and sugar in a bowl until pale and creamy. Place a sieve over the bowl.

Once the cream has come to the boil, pour it through the sieve over the eggs. Discard the pod.

Whisk all the ingredients together, then pour back into the saucepan. Gently heat, whisking constantly, until the custard thickens and coats the back of a spoon. Transfer to a jug, squeeze any excess water from the gelatine, then whisk into the hot custard until melted. Pour into the ramekins and, when cool, refrigerate for at least 6 hours, or overnight.

To release the panna cottas, quickly dip the ramekins into boiling water, then upturn onto a plate.

> **Chef's Tip**
>
> If possible, use vanilla sugar for the panna cotta to add more depth of flavour.

For The Rhubarb Ripple Ice Cream

Place the rhubarb, water and 100g of the sugar in a pan and cook on a low heat to a purée.

Gently bring the cream, milk and vanilla to the boil in a separate pan.

Whisk together the eggs and remaining sugar in a bowl until pale, creamy and doubled in size.

Combine the cream mix with the eggs and pour back into the saucepan. Place the pan over a gentle heat, whisking constantly, until the custard thickens and coats the back of a spoon. Pour into a suitable container and refrigerate. Once chilled, churn in an ice cream machine. Drizzle in the rhubarb purée at the end of churning to create a ripple effect.

To Serve

Simply top the panna cottas with the cooked rhubarb and serve, as pictured, with the rhubarb ripple ice cream.

222
THE WESTWOOD RESTAURANT

New Walk, Beverley, East Yorkshire, HU17 7AE

01482 881 999
www.thewestwood.co.uk Twitter: @The_Westwood Instagram: the_westwood_restaurant

Matthew and Michele Barker focus on offering high quality, locally sourced ingredients, showcasing the best of what the region has to offer.

The Westwood has become one of the most popular restaurants in East Yorkshire, situated in the historic market town of Beverley, between York and Hull. The Westwood is located a short walk from the Westwood Pasture offering stunning views of the Black Mill, the racecourse and Beverley Minster. Set in the grounds of Beverley's former Grade II listed Georgian courthouse, The Westwood's contemporary interior blends beautifully with the period features and charm of this historic building.

For Matthew, cooking is about getting the best out of the ingredients, delivering beautiful plates packed with great flavour. The Westwood believes in making the most of the seasons, so the menu is constantly changing to bring you the best of locally sourced produce - beef sourced from North Yorkshire and seafood caught off Yorkshire's east coast feature heavily.

Enjoy a relaxing meal in modern, elegant surroundings. You can also dine outdoors on the spacious garden terrace during the summer months, or why not start your evening in the W Bar for a pre-dinner cocktail.

Whether you're joining The Westwood for a light lunch, an evening meal or a special occasion, you can always look forward to a warm welcome, a relaxed atmosphere and friendly service.

Photography by Nicholas Bennett www.nicholasbennettdop.com

Listed in the Michelin Guide 2019, Hardens 2019 and holder of 2 AA Rosettes, The Westwood was listed in the Top 100 Best Restaurants in the UK 2018.

CEP MUSHROOM & JERUSALEM ARTICHOKE MACARONI, ARLINGTON WHITE HEN'S EGG, AUTUMN BLACK TRUFFLE

SERVES 4

 Pansa Blanca, Raventós De Alella 2017, Catalonia (Spain)

Ingredients

Mushroom And Jerusalem Artichoke Macaroni

500g macaroni (ditalini)
500g king oyster mushrooms
200g Jerusalem artichokes (peeled)
olive oil (drizzle of)

Jerusalem Artichoke Purée

800g Jerusalem artichokes (peeled)
200ml chicken stock
1 sprig thyme
100ml whipping cream
salt and white pepper (to season)

Cep Sauce

100g dried cep mushrooms
4 large shallots (diced)
3 cloves garlic (peeled, diced)
1 sprig thyme
butter (knob of)
100ml Madeira
400ml chicken stock
100ml whipping cream

Poached Eggs

4 Arlington White eggs
white wine vinegar (splash of)

Garnish

30g black truffle (thinly sliced)
24-month aged Parmesan (grated)
nasturtium leaves

Method

For The Mushroom And Jerusalem Artichoke Macaroni

Blanch the macaroni in salted boiling water for 7 minutes, then refresh in cold water and set aside. Dice the king oyster mushrooms and Jerusalem artichokes to 5mm dice. *Sauté* in a little olive oil for 5 minutes, keeping the mushrooms and artichoke dice *al dente*. Remove from the pan, drain and set aside to cool.

For The Jerusalem Artichoke Purée

Slice the Jerusalem artichokes, reserving 1 for the crisps. Place in a shallow pan with the stock and thyme, cook until tender. When the stock has reduced, add the cream, season with salt and white pepper, then blend to a purée. Pass through a fine sieve and set aside.

> **Chef's Tip**
>
> To add texture, thinly slice some Jerusalem artichokes and deep fry at 180°C until golden brown and crisp.

For The Cep Sauce

Soak the cep mushrooms in boiling water for 20 minutes. *Sauté* the shallots, garlic and thyme in a heavy-based pan in a little butter. Drain the ceps, reserving the mushroom stock. Add the ceps to the pan and *sauté* for a further 5 minutes, then *deglaze* with the Madeira. Pass the mushroom stock through a fine sieve to remove any sediment, then add to the pan. Pour in the chicken stock, reduce by half then add the whipping cream. Bring to the boil, then remove from the heat. Pass through a fine sieve.

For The Poached Eggs

Bring a large pan of salted water with a splash of vinegar to the boil. Whisk the water to form a slow whirlpool. Crack the eggs in one at a time and cook for 3 minutes. You can do this earlier in the day and refresh the eggs in ice cold water. Trim off the excess white and place on a tray in the fridge until needed. Reheat by *blanching* in boiling water.

To Assemble The Dish

Bring the cep sauce to the boil, then add the pasta and artichoke and mushroom mix. Gently reheat the artichoke purée in a separate pan. Place 3-4 tablespoons of pasta in each bowl, followed by 1 tablespoon of artichoke purée. Place the hot poached egg on top of the purée, season with salt and cracked black pepper. Finish with grated Parmesan and thinly sliced black truffle. Plate as pictured with artichoke crisps.

LOIN OF FALLOW DEER, RED CABBAGE, ROASTED CEREAL & GRAINS, BRASSICAS, GAME JUS, BLACKBERRIES

SERVES 4

 Botrosecco, Le Mortelle, Antinori 2015, Tuscany (Italy)

Ingredients

Red Cabbage Purée

90g butter
1 shallot (sliced)
500g red cabbage (thinly sliced)
500ml water
160ml dry red wine
160ml port
160ml red wine vinegar
1 tbsp caster sugar
70ml chicken stock
salt and white pepper

Roasted Cereal And Grains

45g coarse oatmeal
12g sunflower seeds
5g pumpkin seeds
¼ tsp mixed spice
10g soft brown sugar
½ tsp Maldon sea salt
12g golden syrup, 2 tsp honey
1 tsp sunflower oil

Game Jus

2 tbsp redcurrant jelly
1 litre game stock, 500ml red wine
200g tin chopped tomatoes

Loin Of Fallow Deer

1kg fallow deer loin (*larder trimmed*)
salt and pepper, butter (knob of)
rapeseed oil (drizzle of)

To Serve

200g turnip (sliced), chicken stock
500g kale

Garnish

1 punnet blackberries, red chicory leaves

Method

For The Red Cabbage Purée

Heat two-thirds of the butter in a large pan over a medium heat until foaming but not browned. Add the shallot and sweat until soft. Stir in the cabbage and cook for 5 minutes. Season with salt. Add just enough water to cover the cabbage, then place a lid on the pan. Turn the heat to low and cook the cabbage until very soft, about 40 minutes. When the water is nearly evaporated, add the wine and port and bring to a simmer. Reduce the liquid until the pan is nearly dry. Add the vinegar and sugar, reduce until almost dry. Transfer the mixture to a blender and purée on high until smooth. Add the remaining butter and stock. Blend until *emulsified*. Pass through a fine sieve. Season with salt and white pepper.

For The Roasted Cereal And Grains

Preheat the oven to 160°C.

Combine the dry ingredients in a bowl. Heat the honey, syrup and sunflower oil in a pan, then pour the hot liquid over the dry ingredients and mix well. Place on an oven tray lined with greaseproof paper and bake for 25 minutes, stirring every 5 minutes for an even colour. This can be made days in advance; store in an airtight container.

For The Game Jus

Combine the ingredients in a pan and reduce to 500ml. Pass through a fine sieve and set aside.

For The Loin Of Fallow Deer

Preheat the oven to 180°C.

Cut the loin into 4 portions. Season and sear on both sides for 2 minutes in rapeseed oil and butter. Transfer to the oven for 5 minutes, then leave to rest for 6 minutes.

> **Chef's Tip**
>
> Buy the fallow deer from a quality high street butcher. Wild is preferred however farmed is a good alternative.

To Serve

Blanch the turnip in chicken stock until tender. *Sauté* the kale and gently warm the cabbage purée. Plate as pictured.

CHOCOLATE TART, RASPBERRIES, PISTACHIO BRITTLE

SERVES 8-12

🍷 *Maury Grenat, Lafage 2016, Maury
(France)*

Ingredients

Chocolate Tart Case

125g unsalted butter
125g icing sugar
1 tsp cooking salt
1 whole egg
1 egg yolk
250g plain flour
50g cocoa powder

Chocolate Filling

260g dark chocolate (70%)
250g milk chocolate (33%)
200ml double cream
300ml whole milk
2 tsp salt
150g whole eggs

Pistachio Brittle

150g sugar
45g butter
32g glucose syrup
45ml water
2g baking soda
6g salt
130g pistachios (toasted)

To Serve

3 punnets raspberries
milk ice cream or crème fraîche

23cm non-stick loose-bottomed tart case
non-stick baking mat

Method

For The Chocolate Tart Case

Cream the butter, sugar and salt in a mixer using a 'K' beater. Add the egg and yolk and continue mixing, then add the flour and cocoa powder and mix to form a dough. Wrap the dough in cling film and chill for 2 hours.

Preheat the oven to 170°C.

Roll the pastry to 5mm thick and carefully transfer to the tart case. Line with 3 layers of cling film, add baking beans and blind bake for 20 minutes. Remove the beans and cook for a further 8 minutes. Remove from the oven and leave to cool. Turn the oven temperature down to 90°C.

For The Chocolate Filling

Place the chocolate in a metal bowl. Heat the cream, milk and salt to a simmer, then pour over the chocolate and combine. Whisk the eggs slightly, then mix into the chocolate mix. Pour into the tart case, return to the oven and cook for 1 hour until set. Leave to cool.

For The Pistachio Brittle

Heat the sugar, butter, glucose and water over a medium heat until it becomes golden. Stir in the baking soda and salt, then add the nuts. Turn out onto a non-stick mat and leave to cool. When totally cooled, blitz in a food processor to form a crumb. Reserve in an airtight container.

To Serve

Slice the tart with a warm, sharp knife. Arrange the raspberries on top. Finish with pistachio crumb and serve with milk ice cream or crème fraîche.

> **Chef's Tip**
>
> To create the chocolate twigs, pipe *tempered*, melted dark chocolate into an iced water bath, then remove and leave to dry. Dust with cocoa powder to finish.

RELISH NORTH EAST & YORKSHIRE LARDER

FISH

CARRICKS FISH LTD
Yew Tree House, Snape, North Yorkshire, DL8 2TJ.
T: 01677 470 499 www.carricksfish.co.uk
Supplier of fish and shellfish, as well as local fruit and vegetables.

HODGSON FISH
5 Whitby Street, Hartlepool, TS24 7AD.
T: 01429 273 169 www.hodgsonfish.co.uk
Established in 1916, Hodgson fish is by far the most experienced wholesaler of fish and seafood in Yorkshire and the North East. Their ethos is simple: to supply the freshest sustainable fish to their clients, prepared to the highest specification, without compromise. What makes them special is their unique supply chain, often able to have product from trawler to table within 20 hours, beautifully prepared and packed for the most discerning customers.

LINDISFARNE SEAFOODS LTD
2 Cliffords Fort, North Shields, Tyne and Wear, NE30 1JE.
T: 0191 259 2909 www.fish-quay.com
Suppliers of the finest variety of crabs, langoustines, lobsters and shellfish on the North Shields Fish Quay.

RR FOWLER & SON – BURNHOLME FISHERIES
1 Gerard Avenue, Burnholme, York, YO31 0QT.
T: 01904 421 360 www.fowlersofyork.co.uk
By purchasing fish from markets up and down the east coast of England, and from ports both in the UK and internationally, they have the ability to bring together all manner of seafood of only the highest quality, to be delivered fresh to your door.

SWALLOW FISH LTD
'The Fisherman's Kitchen', 2 South Street, Seahouses, Northumberland, NE68 7RB.
T: 01665 721 052 www.swallowfish.co.uk
The last fully operational 19th Century smokehouse in Seahouses, where they smoke kippers, salmon and fish in the traditional way.

WHITBY CATCH
1 Pier Road, Whitby, North Yorkshire, YO21 3PT.
T: 01947 601 313 www.thewhitbycatch.co.uk
The Whitby Catch Online Shop, Whitby's first and only online fish and seafood ordering service! All fish and seafood is prepared to your individual requirement.

WINES & BEERS

BERKMANN WINE CELLAR
16 Marston Moor Business Park, Rudgate, Tockwith, North Yorkshire, YO26 7QF.
T: 01423 357 567 www.berkmann.co.uk

DURHAM BREWERY
Unit 6a Bowburn North Industrial Estate, Bowburn, Durham, Co Durham, DH6 5PF.
T: 0191 377 1991 www.durhambrewery.co.uk
Selection of artisan beers.

NEWHOUSE & CO WINE MERCHANTS
LEVENSDALE HOUSE
Ayton Road, Stokesley, North Yorkshire, TS9 5JW.
T: 01642 714 046 www.newhouseandco.co.uk
Offering a range of wines from across the globe.

234
RELISH NORTH EAST
& YORKSHIRE LARDER

MEAT & POULTRY

BLACKWELL'S BUTCHERS
Norton High Street, Stockton-on-Tees, TS20 1DS.
T: 01624 559 191 www.blackwells-butchers.co.uk
Blackwell's since 1954
*Multi award-winning Blackwell's Butchers, have
been providing the local community with the finest
quality meats for over half a century. Nestled in the
heart of Norton Village, Blackwell's Butchers are an
integral part of the local community and village life
and are strongly committed to not only providing the
very best produce available but also protecting the
heritage and maintaining the character of Norton.*

*All the staff are happy to serve and advise on all
aspects of meat preparation, the best cooking
methods and the most appropriate cuts to ensure
you leave the shop with exactly what you need for
the perfect meal - every time!*

FREEMAN BUTCHERS
353A Dukesway Court, Team Valley Trading Estate,
Gateshead, Tyne and Wear, NE11 0BH.
T: 0191 456 0297 www.freemanbutchers.co.uk

J D HALLS
2 Hill Street, Corbridge, NE45 5AA.
T: 01434 632 005
*Top drawer butcher supplying delicious cuts and
very, very tasty black pudding.*

FARMISON & CO
Charter Road, Canalside, Ripon HG4, 1AJ.
T: 01765 824 050 www.farmison.com
*Farmison & Co are a specialist butcher and game
dealer, supplying the very best Yorkshire has to offer;
named breeds from individually named farms.*

LISHMAN'S OF ILKLEY AWARD-WINNING YORKSHIRE BUTCHERS

25 Leeds Road, Ilkley, West Yorkshire, LS29 8DP.
T: 01943 609 436 www.lishmansbutchers.co.uk
Lishman's of Ilkley is a multi award-winning butcher in the spa town of Ilkley, nestled at the gateway to the Yorkshire Dales. Sourcing the majority of meat from established Yorkshire farms, Lishman's supports regional farmers who share their commitment to welfare and outstanding quality. Provenance is paramount at Lishman's; almost everything in the shop is prepared entirely in-house with particular renown for exceptional sausages, bacon, hams and homemade pies.

R&J YORKSHIRE'S FINEST FARMERS AND BUTCHERS

Water Edge, Longswales Lane, Ripon, HG4 3RR.
T: 01765 658 611 www.randjyorkshiresfinest.co.uk
Well aged and matured meat delivered daily from a family run business (est 1978) supplying high quality meat to catering establishments throughout Yorkshire. They produce, farm, fatten and sell their own beef and lamb and also supply a full range of pork, chicken, duck, game and traditional handmade sausages. All sourced from local farms and estates within a 15 mile radius and prepared fresh daily for customers.

THREE LITTLE PIGS

Kiplingcotes Farm, Dalton Holme, Beverley, HU17 7PY.
T: 07910 315 956 www.threelittlepigschorizo.co.uk
Three Little Pigs is a perfectionist award-winning producer of cured meats based in Yorkshire, making hand finished chorizo and salami from rare breed pigs.

DAIRY

DELIFRESH

59-62 St James's Market, Essex Street, Bradford, West Yorkshire, BD4 7PG.
T: 01274 743 737 delifreshltd.co.uk
Delifresh are passionate about fresh produce, dairy, cheese and speciality flavours. They deliver into kitchens throughout the north of the UK on a daily basis.

G G BAYNES & SON

Marley Cote Walls, Slaley, Hexham, NE47 0DQ.
T: 01434 673 244 www.marleycote.co.uk
Northumberland pedigree milk and cream.

RELISH NORTH EAST
& YORKSHIRE LARDER

MATTHEWS CHEESE

23-24 Grainger Arcade, Grainger Market, Newcastle
T: 0191 232 4265
*Continental and English cheese. Over 150 of the
finest quality cheeses to choose from. Also a large
selection of herbs, spices and a selection of
flavoured nuts.*

MICHAEL LEE FINE CHEESES

Unit 9 Lister Park, Green Lane Industrial Estate,
Featherstone, West Yorkshire, WF7 6FE.
T: 01977 703 061 www.finecheesesltd.co.uk
*Fast growing specialist B2B wholesalers, supplying a
vast selection of gourmet cheeses, charcuterie, meat
products, tapas and chef's store cupboard items.*

*Sourced direct from artisan manufacturers,
importing from across the world and maturing
cheeses in-house.*

*Weekly and next day deliveries throughout Yorkshire
and further afield. Personal consultation with
Michael Lee available upon request. Their extensive
experience of retail and wholesale markets keeps
Michael Lee Fine Cheeses as a leading wholesaler.*

NORTHUMBERLAND CHEESE COMPANY

The Cheese Farm, Green Lane, Blagdon,
Northumberland, NE13 6BZ.
T: 01670 789 798
www.northumberlandcheese.co.uk
*Award-winning Northumberland cheeses made to
traditional recipes by a small, hands-on, dedicated
team. Established in 1984 by Mark Robertson and
based in a small dairy on the Blagdon Estate, they
hand-make, wrap and sell a range of 16 cheeses
including cow, sheep, goat and Jersey. They may be
small, but they have a big passion for handcrafting
fine cheese. Every mouthful can be traced back to a
single local dairy herd, it's all part of the
Northumberland Cheese Company philosophy.*

PARLOUR MADE ARTISAN CHEESE
Village Farm Dairy, Morden, Sedgefield, TS21 2EY.
T: 01740 622 255 www.parlourmade.co.uk

PEXTENEMENT CHEESE COMPANY LTD
Eastwood, Todmorden, OL14 8RW.
T: 07725 517 934 www.pextenement.co.uk

SHEPHERD'S PURSE
Leachfield Grange, Newsham, Thirsk,
North Yorkshire, YO7 4DJ.
T: 01845 587 220 www.shepherdspurse.co.uk
*Shepherd's Purse is a small, family run, artisan
cheese company producing the finest, traditional
and continental style cheeses on their farm in
North Yorkshire.*

FINE & SPECIALITY FOODS

BLAGDON FARM SHOP
16-18 Milkhope Centre, Blagdon, Newcastle upon
Tyne, NE13 6DA.
*T: 01670 789 924 www.theblagdonfarmshop.co.uk
Award-winning butcher's shop and traditional
farmhouse kitchen selling Blagdon's own produced
beef, pork and poultry, freshly picked and local
farm produce.*

BURTREE PUDDINGS
Burtree House, Burtree Lane, Nr Darlington, DL3 0UY.
T: 01325 463 521 www.burtreepuddings.co.uk
*Home of the sticky toffee pudding! All puddings are
made with absolutely the finest ingredients from
free range eggs, English butter and of course, their
neighbouring organic dairy farm's double cream.*

CRYER AND STOTT
Station Road, Allerton Bywater, Castleford,
West Yorkshire, WF10 2BP.
T: 01977 510 638 www.cryerandstott.co.uk
*Situated in both Pontefract and Castleford's
Market Halls, Cryer and Stott Pontefract and
Castleford are run as a franchise by Richard's
brother Stuart.*

*The shops sell a wide selection of cheese, cooked
meats, cured bacon, gammons, and freshly baked
award-winning pork pies. They also have a fresh
delivery of locally baked bread each day. On the
shelving you'll find a mouthwatering range of
chutneys, pickles and jams; and carry a gourmet
range of foods from around the world.*

RELISH NORTH EAST & YORKSHIRE LARDER

DELI FRESH
Kingsway North, Team Valley, Gateshead, NE1 1OS.
T: 0191 487 6177
Supplies bespoke regional fresh produce daily. If you ever need that little something different, they will source it for you.

MILLER FOOD SERVICE
David Miller Frozen Foods Ltd, 27 Hospital Fields Road, York, YO10 4DZ.
T: 01904 655 368 www.millerfoodservice.co.uk
Miller Food Service supply all dry goods such as spices etc.

UDALE SPECIALITY FOODS
1-3 Schola Green Lane, Morecambe LA4 5QT.
T: 01524 411 611 www.udale.com
Udale Speciality Foods is a family owned business run by brothers, Ian and Neil Udale. The company was founded by their great grandfather in 1905.

Their list of awards included: 'Best Lamb', 'Best Beef', 'Best Pork', 'Venison Sausage', 'Pork and Chutney Pie', and for those with a sweet tooth, 'Luxury Vanilla Pod Ice Cream'.

WELLOCKS
4 Pendleside, Nelson, Lancashire, BB9 6SH.
T: 08444 993 444 www.wellocks.co.uk
Wellocks provide fruit, vegetables, dairy, poultry, meat, sundries, store cupboard essentials and everything else you'll need. And for ingredients that are even more extraordinary, there's their growing 'Special Branch' collection.

VEGETABLES AND FRUIT

TIM PYBUS, VILLAGE FARM
Main Street, West Tanfield, Ripon, North Yorkshire, HG4 5JJ.
T: 01677 470 340
Supplier of delicious free-range eggs.

Award-winning Alnwick Gin is handcrafted with love in the heart of rural Northumberland. Created using a secret recipe and made using the finest botanicals, including juniper, lavender, fennel and rosehip. Prepare yourself for an incredibly smooth and surprising taste sensation.

Why not also enjoy the warmth of Northumberland in a bottle with their handcrafted sloe gin. Created using the finest, handpicked Northumberland sloe berries blended with natural sloe juice to give an outstanding finish.

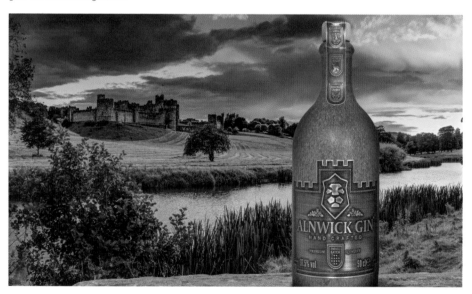

For trade enquiries please contact Ian Woods, Sales Director on 01665 579 100 or email ian@northumberlandspirit.co.uk

Alnwick Gin, Northumberland Spirit Company, Blacksmiths Hall, Rock, Alnwick, NE66 3SB.

www.alnwickgin.co.uk

AL DENTE

Al dente describes vegetables that are cooked to the 'tender crisp' phase - still offering resistance to the bite, but cooked through. Al dente can also describe cooked pasta which is firm but not hard.

BAIN-MARIE

A pan or other container of hot water with a bowl placed on top of it. This allows the steam from the water to heat the bowl so ingredients can be gently heated or melted.

BEURRE NOISETTE

Unsalted butter is melted over a low heat until it begins to caramelise and brown. When it turns a nutty colour, it should be removed from the heat to stop it burning. Can be used as a base for butter sauces or added to cakes and batters.

BLANCH

Boiling an ingredient before removing it and plunging it in ice cold water in order to stop the cooking process.

BRUNOISE

A type of culinary cut in which food is diced into quarter inch (3.175mm) cubes. The formal-looking little squares add colour and elegance to dishes.

CARTOUCHE

A piece of greaseproof paper that covers the surface of a stew, soup, stock or sauce to reduce evaporation.

CHINOIS

A conical sieve with an extremely fine mesh. It is used to strain custards, purées, soups and sauces, producing a very smooth texture.

CLARIFIED BUTTER

Milk fat rendered from butter to separate the milk solids and water from the butter fat.

CONFIT

A method of cooking where the meat is cooked and submerged in a liquid to add flavour. Often this liquid is rendered fat. Confit can also apply to fruits - fruit confits are cooked and preserved in sugar, the result is like candied fruits.

DEGLAZE

To make a gravy or sauce by adding liquid to the cooking juices and food particles in a pan in which meat or other ingredients have been cooked.

EMULSION/EMULSIFY

In the culinary arts, an emulsion is a mixture of two liquids that would ordinarily not mix together, like oil and vinegar.

FRENCH TRIM

Fat, meat or skin is cut away to expose a piece of bone, so that it sticks out. It also means that any excess fat is cut off. French Trimming can be done to lamb chops and bigger cuts; it can even can be done to chicken legs or breasts.

JULIENNE

A culinary knife cut in which the vegetable is sliced into long thin strips, similar to matchsticks.

LARDER TRIMMED

The term given to steaks which have been trimmed to leave only the eye of the steak. This cut is often used in a beef Wellington.

LIQUOR

The liquid that is left over from the cooking of meat or vegetables. Can be incorporated into sauces and gravy.

MACERATED

Raw, dried or preserved fruit and vegetables soaked in a liquid to soften the food or to absorb the flavour.

MIREPOIX

Finely diced combination of celery (pascal, celery or celeriac), onions and carrots. There are many regional mirepoix variations, which can sometimes be just one of these ingredients, or include additional spices creating a rich, flavoursome base to sauces or stews.

NAGE

A term for a flavoured liquid used for poaching delicate foods, typically seafood. A traditional nage is a broth flavoured with white wine, vegetables and herbs, in which seafood is poached. The liquid is then reduced and thickened with cream and/or butter.

PANE

To coat with flour, beaten egg and breadcrumbs for deep frying.

QUENELLE

A neat, three-sided oval (resembling a mini rugby ball) that is formed by gently smoothing the mixture between two dessertspoons.

ROCHER

A one-handed quenelle.

SABAYON

Made by beating egg yolks with a liquid over simmering water until thickened and increased in volume. The liquid can be water, but Champagne or wine is often used.

SAUTE

To fry in a small amount of fat.

SOUS VIDE

French for 'under vacuum.' A method of cooking food sealed in airtight plastic bags in a water bath or in a temperature-controlled steam environment for longer than normal cooking times. The intention is to cook the item evenly, ensuring that the inside is properly cooked without overcooking the outside, and to retain moisture.

TEMPER

To temper eggs is to add a hot liquid to an egg mixture without cooking the eggs. Tempering is to slowly bring up the temperature of the eggs without scrambling them. Tempering also refers to a process of heating and cooling chocolate to prepare it for dipping and enrobing. The tempering process ensures a smooth texture, a glossy shine and a pleasant 'snap' when bitten or broken.

ALL THE INGREDIENTS FOR YOUR RECIPE TO SUCCESS

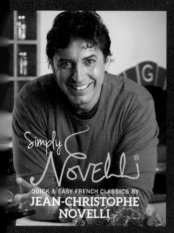

Relish is proud to have worked with more than 1500 of the UK's best-loved chefs to showcase their wonderful restaurants and food but there is a huge appetite for more.

Mark Greenaway and Jean Christophe Novelli are just two of the industry's leading lights who worked with our small, professional and dedicated team to produce their own beautiful books - stamped with their personality and signature dishes.

Mark's book Perceptions was named the world's best chef cookbook at the Gourmand World Cookbook Awards. It is an amazing accolade and testament to Mark's passion for the art and the wonderful natural larder he works with. Perceptions is an outstanding example of how, as an independent publisher, we are able to focus on you, your restaurant and your region to showcase culinary excellence to our readers who are always hungry to try out new dishes.

Owning this book is just for starters, reading it is the main course. Why not go for dessert and let us help you create a bespoke publication of your own to share with your loyal customers and attract new fans along the way? You will be on the shelves alongside our fantastic portfolio of beautifully illustrated guides, which are stocked nationally in Waterstones, Harvey Nichols, in each featured restaurant, in leading independent stores and online globally. You could be the next published chef to join the world's elite

Relish has a small, friendly, professional team, with experience in publishing, print management, editing, proofing, photography, design and artwork, sales distribution and marketing. We ensure a personal approach, working exceptionally hard to develop a great product which reflects each chef's talent and passion.

Duncan and Teresa Peters established the company in 2009, with a vision of building a niche publishing house for food lovers. The success of Relish Publications is reflected in the fact that we are the UK's leading regional recipe book publisher.

To book a personal consultation with our friendly, dedicated team contact our head

"Relish books are full of enjoyable recipes and ideas for making the most of the edible treasures we have on our doorstep; both places to eat them and new, exciting ways to cook them."

Angela Hartnett, MBE

"The Relish cookbook offers the home cook some great inspiration to make the most of these wonderful ingredients in season."

Tom Kitchin

"With mouthwatering, easy to follow recipes and beautiful photography, Relish South West is a must have for any foodie, from professional chef to the inspired home cook."

Michael Caines MBE

"This book showcases some extremely hardworking chefs. Enjoy their recipes and the inspiration behind them but, best of all, go and discover their restaurants, taste what they do and experience some great northern hospitality."

Michael Wignall

"Relish Midlands is a fantastic recipe book that brings together so many of the talented chefs and quality restaurants in the area. It gives you a taste of what our exciting region has to offer as well as the encouragement to try some new recipes."

Adam Stokes

"Relish Wales is a fabulous way to showcase some of our beautiful country's fabulous eateries and to be able to share our food with a wider audience."

Stephen Terry

AVAILABLE TO BUY IN OUR FEATURED RESTAURANTS & IN ALL GOOD BOOKSHOPS

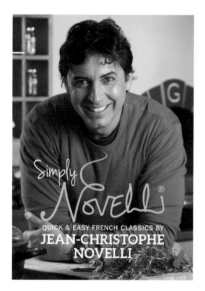

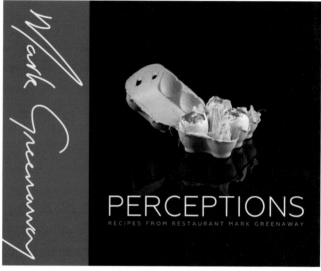

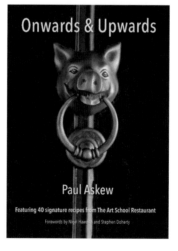

Relish
SCOTLAND
Original recipes from Scotland's finest chefs and restaurants. Introduction by chef Geoffrey Smeddle.

FOURTH EDITION

Relish
SOUTH WEST
Original recipes from the South West's finest chefs and restaurants. Introduction by Michael Caines MBE.

Relish
NORTH EAST & YORKSHIRE
Original recipes from the regions' best-loved chefs and restaurants. Introduction by chef patron Michael Wignall.

THIRD EDITION

Relish
NORTH WEST
SECOND HELPING
Original recipes from the region's finest chefs and restaurants. Introduction by chef Paul Askew.

Relish
MIDLANDS
SECOND HELPING
Original recipes from the region's finest chefs and restaurants. Introduction by Adam Stokes.

Relish
WALES
Original recipes from the region's finest chefs and restaurants. Introduction by chef Will Holland.

THIRD EDITION

HOW TO MAKE ICE CREAM WITHOUT A MACHINE

Although relatively inexpensive these days, not everyone has access to an ice cream machine. That's no reason not to follow some of these delicious recipes found in the Relish North East & Yorkshire book. Although more time consuming than a machine, excellent results can be obtained by following this simple method.

Follow the recipe right up until it tells you to churn in the machine, including any chilling time in the fridge.

Take your mixture from the fridge and stir with a rubber spatula. Transfer it to a suitable plastic container with a lid. There should be at least 2cm space at the top to allow the mixture to expand when freezing. Cover and place in the freezer for two hours.

Remove from the freezer and beat with a hand mixer, still in the container, to break up the ice crystals that are beginning to form. Cover and return to the freezer for a further 2 hours. (If you don't have a hand mixer then you may use a fork and some 'elbow grease' to break up the crystals).

Remove from the freezer and beat again with the hand mixer. The ice cream should be thickening up nicely at this point but too soft to scoop. Return it to the freezer for an additional hour. Beat again. If your ice cream is still not thickened sufficiently, repeat this process again after another hour. When the ice cream has thickened properly, stir in any add-ins at this point (honeycomb, nuts...). Do not beat with the hand mixer after the add-ins have been mixed in.

Place the tightly sealed container in the freezer and allow the ice cream to freeze until firm. The ice cream should be removed from the freezer 15-20 minutes before you wish to eat it. This will make scooping easier.

This method will also work for sorbets. Sometimes sorbets may go a bit 'icy' or 'crumbly' if left for too long in the freezer. This can be rectified by blitzing in a food processor just before serving.

Peanut Butter Mousse, Banana, Raspberry - **Page 200**

HOW TO MAKE A SUGAR STOCK SYRUP

This makes about 750ml sugar stock. It can be stored in a sterilised jar in the fridge for a couple of months.

500g white sugar
500ml water

Place the sugar and water in a pan. Dissolve slowly over a very low heat. You must not allow the syrup to boil until all the sugar has dissolved, about 5 minutes. Once completely dissolved, bring to the boil, then simmer for 5 minutes.

CONVERSION CHART

COOKING TEMPERATURES

Degrees Celsius	Fahrenheit	Gas Mark
140	275	1
150	300	2
160-170	325	3
180	350	4
190	375	5
200-210	400	6
220	425	7
230	450	8
240	475	9

*Temperatures for fan-assisted ovens are, as a general rule, normally about 20°C lower than regular oven temperatures.

WEIGHT MEASUREMENT CONVERSIONS

1 teaspoon (5ml/5g)	$^1/_4$ oz
1 tablespoon (15ml/15g)	$^3/_4$ oz
10g	$^1/_2$ oz
25g	1oz
50g	2oz
75g	3oz
150g	5oz
200g	7oz
250g	9oz
350g	12oz
450g	1lb
1kg	2.2lb

VOLUME MEASUREMENT CONVERSIONS

55ml	2 fl oz
150ml	$^1/_4$ pt
275ml	$^1/_2$ pt
570ml	1 pt
1 litre	$1^3/_4$ pt